JARGON 58

PATAGONI
Paul Metcalf

The Jargon Society
Penland, North Carolina
1971

This project is supported by a grant
from the *National Endowment for the Arts* in Washington, D.C.,
a Federal agency created by Act of Congress in 1965.

Manufactured in the United States of America by
Heritage Printers, Inc., Charlotte, North Carolina

Designed by Jonathan Williams, who is also responsible
for the montage. Credit and thanks are due to the
collections of the Henry Ford Museum and Greenfield
Village; Wide World Photos, Inc.; LIFE Magazine
(Dmitri Kessel and Co Rentmeester), copyright by Time,
Inc.; and *Maize in the Great Herbals,* J. J. Finan.
Waltham, Mass., 1950.

Special thanks to Bernard Rands, Lyons Music Centre,
University of York, Heslington, Yorkshire, England
for his presentation of the Peruvian folk-music scores.

Distributed by
Small Publishers' Company,
276 Park Avenue South
New York, New York 10010

CONTENTS

DARLINGTON,
SOUTH CAROLINA

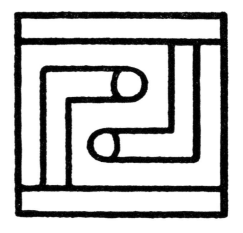

the modern south—pine barrens of lowcountry south carolina, where space appears to go on forever—is not at all unlike modern midwest:

where the land is flat, there is so much of everything to be seen: all that is green lies open, and the blue is cosmic, a true half-shell, full of yesterday's and tomorrow's and everybody else's thunderheads . . .

against this, darlington: labor day, the southern 500, stands and infield jammed, eighty thousand, like the sunday market at huancayo, the plaza filled with indians—americans gone mad with color and shape, shirts, hats, helmets, parasols—the biggest stock car race of them all

knifing around and through, the black oval: the track—the pitcrews all in white, cardoctors: black & white, asphalt & speed . . .

> black fords on
> black tires on
> black-ass
> fault

the cars in idiot pursuit of one another, round and round, all in line to catch the highbank turn, chomping butyl, gorging gas, puffing smoke—the chuff-chuff of lawrence's whitman . . .

when the man ahead is too slow, you can't pass, you bump him, hinting, at better than 100 m.p.h. . . .

and the wrecks: a tire blows (track temperature: 130°) and the car hurtles the guard rail, rolls out of sight—or spins and backs to a halt in midtrack, spews burning gas down the bank of the turn, the driver helpless, rest of the field coming at him, at better than 100 (when bobby myers got his, the one car hurtled straight in the air, smashed by another before it came down: the motor torn from the body, violent and then quiet)

[3]

heavy limbed I
rush to that space

where I will crash
and burn
and scatter steel and gas

and limbs will crush
for want of air, butyl
equilibrium

and heavy footed men
will pass

but it is carnival, and the white souls who came down the day before, drove their pickup trucks into the infield, built their raffish scaffolds, platforms and tents, camped the night, drank their beer and fried their eggs, boiled all day in the sun of better than a hundred—are tired: quiet-like, they take down their rigs, start their motors, begin to file out, slow, tunneling under the track, before the race is over; this is carnival, a holiday, but next day is work day; they go out like sheep, like huancayo llamas, under the track, the motors silent against the unmuffled thunder above...

TIHUANACU

ONE

a.

the humboldt current moves northward, hugging the coast of chile and peru, the bottom waters, polar waters, upwelling

subantartic into subtropical, juxtaposed—as climates slice each other, as jungle, mountain and desert dispose themselves, on the adjacent land

bottom waters upwelling, turbid with plankton, a thick soup for herring, mackeral and pilchard, these a pasturage for seal and porpoise, cormorant and penguin, petrel, kelp gull

plankton and crustacea, dead and dying, rain out of the churning, to feed the forests of rooted animals at the bottom, the bottom-living fish

the waters turning, cool, flow northward, swarm with whale and anchoveta,

> bonito, preying from beneath, the surface hissing as the ancho-veta leaps

> ojo de uva

> rockpool fishes, schooling, planktonfeeding forms, freeswimming sharks

> dogfish ratfish skate ray and silversides

> the liza, stranded on the flats of paracas, corvina, at the flooding river mouths

borracho (a blenny) producing, when eaten, stupefaction, and

the cusk eel

and over these the birds! the thunderheads, the snakeshape clouds passing, passing, daylong clouds

cormorants diving, plunging, fishgorging at the surface

the gannets diving from a height, a barrage of boobies, the ocean a thick
foam as they strike, fish and rise

a booby squall, darkening the sky, spots a fish school—brought thick by
upwelling waters to the surface—and the squall drops, vanishes, as one
bird

there are camanay, alcatraz, piquero, and the guanay, kin to the blue-
eyed shag, the rock shag, a circumpolar bird, panantarctic, swarming
northward with the fishrich current

pelicans, gulls and guanayes, gorging, driving the silversides beyond the
tideline, on the shore

at sunset, the crisscrossing lines of birds, filing to their islands, snowwhite
islands black with birds, the air thick with mutterings, the hum of wings,
grunts and screepy calls

      the birds, the water fowl, circling and dropping
      snowfall upon snowfall, droppings of
      guano snow, circling on the islands

the newfallen guano white, the older, in the glacial depths, a gray, a
brown, an oxide red—thick on the rainless islands, under the rain shadow,
the rainless ceja de la costa

[8]

b.

into this pasturage plunged the indian

mounted his caballito, his bundle of reeds, and straddled, rising to cut
through the breakers, and paddled—or lay on his breast, sculled, the
waters washing over him

he swam with a cluster of calabashes, gourds

or mounted a float made of "skinnes of sea-wolves, blowne vp with winde,"
the seams carefully sewn, with an opening above water, and a small hose,
"and from time to time they did blowe them like balles of winde"

or sailed on a raft of balsas—the pacific washing through—far out to
sea, to fish

c.

the first indian, at the foot of the land, hunted the ground sloth and the
native horse, took pilchards and olave fishes, cooked, there in tierra del
fuego, on a wood that burned sweet, took the wild celery, cress and pars-
nip, the young shoots of tussock, ate mussel, seal, porpoise, cormorant
—whale, crab, gull and penguin.

later, when magellan came, there was "a Man of a prodigious Height,
who was got upon a Hill, to see the Ships pass by," and there were others
of 15 spans, and another that "was fo bygge, that the heade of one of owr
men of a meane ftature, came but to his wafte"

[9]

"Such as measured their footesteppes in the sande, affirme with greate othes, that one theyr feete is almost as longe as twoo feete of owre men of the meane sorte," and

"The Capitayne named thefe people *Patagoni*"

d.

there were others, who sailed down the coast from the north on a fleet of balsas, landing in peru at tumbez and puerto viejo, a race of naked Giants: their knees reached to the natives' heads, their own heads were mountains, hair to the shoulders, eyes the size of plates

plunging their hands into the living rock, they dug wells, spiral, deep, and the water came up fresh

they ravaged the desert valleys for food, strode and rafted into the ocean to take the tiburon and other large fish

they were without women, and used the native female, the gigantic member killing her in the act, until, the number of females reduced, they turned to one another, and plunged the big fish into the living flesh

the Sin of Zodome

drugged, addicted, like the clayeaters of the jungle, a circle of giants rocked on the brown sand, beneath the andes

[10]

e.

on the hot shores, the indian and his woman rolled, rollicked in the sand,
and his phallus—like the serpentphallus of chavín, flashing flower petals
—presented the seed to her lips

she kissed him, and the seed passed once more between them

in semen, sweat and sea air, the indian and his woman performed, mounted the positions

f.

"These two elements [land and water] have one spheare divided between
them, and entertaine and embrace one another in a thousend sortes and
maners. In some places the water encounters the land furiously as an
enemy, and in other places it invirons it after a sweete and amiable man-
ner. There are partes whereas the sea enters far within the land, as coming to visite it; and in other partes the land makes restitution, casting his
capes, points, and tongues farre into the sea, piercing into the bowelles
thereof. In some partes one element ends and another beginnes, yeelding
by degrees one vnto another. In some places, where they ioyne, it is ex-
ceeding deepe . . . "

[11]

alluvial fans, terraces and deltas, narrow plains, and uplifted wavecut shelves . . . and in places, rocks, steep islands, the guano islands, marine frontier of the andes

g.

maya type, or coclé, the chimu came out of the ocean and built chan-chan

in the mountains above the city they turned the waters of the moche, graded them the length of the valley, constructed cisterns and stonelined channels, carried the water, by intricate distribution, into the city itself

out of the gravel, the dry, nitrous sand, they built walls, mounds, terraces, marking the courses of the walls, in the building, with desert reeds

from the moche waters gardens sprang up, the plain became lush, greenery and flowers were tended in the public gardens and the chimu's patios, the walls were carved and painted in designs, houses were built with pitched roofs, terraced roofs of cane, totora—verandas, supported by the twisted algorroba timbers—patios, terraces, all open, so that the gran chimu, in his house open and facing the pacific, sat immersed in his element, counterpart of fish-in-ocean: the chimu in the sea air

on pots and walls:

serpent, lizard, lobster, monkey
                      snakebird, turtle
                                skate, crab and plumed
snail
       birdman, sea bird, cactus—centipede soldier, magic bean soldier, puma, pumabird, the hummingbird soldier

                              guano bird, crabsnake, hun-
dredfooted lobsterserpent

> the moon rules all elements, controls disturbances in the sea,
> makes thunder and lightning, brews the dew that causes crops
> to grow, is greater than the sun because he appears in the sky
> both day and night

offerings of maizemeal, white, were made to the sea

> > pachacamac, built on an eminence on the bank of the
> > rio lurin, turned its back, like chan-chan, to the rising
> > sun, and faced the pacific, the beat of the breakers never
> > out of hearing . . . the fishgod structure was filled with
> > "Figures of divers sorts of Fish", and when an Indian
> > died, the eyes were extracted from the skull, replaced
> > by eyes of the cuttlefish

at chan-chan, the moche waters flowed in the gardens, the flowers
flourished

the sea "threw up vast quantities of Pilchards, with the Heads of which
they dunged their Lands," and the maize came up two crops a year,
"and they have great Plenty of it, and of Beans and Lupins, with which,
and the Fifth they take, they drive a Trade among the People on the
Mountains, and are always rich"

the chimu sat on his patio, beneath a totora veranda, cooled by the south
breeze, his drinking waters potterycooled

[13]

TWO

a.

east of illimani, chimborazo, huascarán, the andean rivers burst the
mountains . . . at the puncu de manseriche, the marañon tumbles out

and a man among snow and thunder, plunging through drift banks, over
slabs of ice, comes up below on the sod, in a jungle sun

      snowwater drips off him, the honeybee swarms, kiss-flowers
      flash among heliconias, palm fronds, airfed orchids

      the bittern, the snowy heron are in the roundwaters, the fishcow
      browses among riveredge herbs

seeds of wild fig dropped by birds in a crotch take root the young fig
shoots down forking reaching for soil forking new shoots like cuttlefish-
tentacles push up hook and strangle
                        lianas run to the branchends fall to
the soil bounce to a new host or reach over riveredges hook and grasp an
indian his raft floating downstream from under him
                              the beanpod of the
ingás grows an armlength
           an indian child rafts the waters on a lily leaf
                                    rain
falls in grape drops toadstools burst
                    brazil nuts crash from the trees snap-
ping branches killing indians beneath
                    the dying palm collapses cracking

like musketshot
        termites grind timber to pulp
                mucor covers the humus

b.

there were men with an eye in the centre of the forehead, others with dogs' heads, and mouths below their stomachs

juan alvarez maldonado found two pigmies and a man five yards in height, with snout and fangs

"Bien adentro destas montañas había unas monas que parían monstruos que tenían las cabezas y miembros deshonestos como hombres y las manos y pies como mona. Esos monstruos eran hijos de los aborigenes" and others tell of indians with monkeytails, and the woman who would not sell her pet black potbellied coata monkey because he was her husband

c.

the centipede is a dog

the red grasshopper a hummingbird

the beetle is a flying mudturtle

[15]

the butterfly a bird

the snake of the bolivian yungas, or the amazon catfish, will eat an indian

the spider a sparrow

the lizard walks upright, like a man

there are "battes as bygge as turtle dooues"—"exceadynge great Tor-
toyfes"—"fpiders of marueylous bygneffe. And I haue feene fumme
with the body and legges, bygger than a mannes hande extended euery
waye. And I ones fawe one of fuche bygneffe, that onely her bodye was
as bygge as a fparrowe, and full of that laune whereof they make their
webbes. This was of a darke ruffette coloure, with ehes greater than
the eies of a fparow"

d.

bushmasters whine in their sleep, the anaconda wails, there is owl laugh-
ter, bullfrogs clang in the ironworks or bray as mules, the steamwhistle
cicada is from a baldwin locomotive, macaws and parrots drown waterfalls

the oxbird bellows like a bull

e.

the monkey's face reddens with passion, hummingbirds, crests erected, fight in midair

at the riveredge, the jaguar, at his leisure, eats the tail of the living alligator, or snarls, in the forest, over avocados

caterpillars go to bitters, bees and wasps are doped and drunk

pigbirds squat on a low branch motionless

the anaconda's breath is foetid, stupefying, and "In the frefh Water Rivers there are extraordinary large Alligators, and the *Portuguefes* fay their Tefticles fmell ftronger than Musk"

f.

the top of the jungle forest is an ocean surface, and, submarine, subarboreal, the indian slips along the bottom, a deepwater fish—or a blind foraging ant, creeping under fallen leaves and branches

he eats the marl, a milky clay—chicken gull stew—and puts his lips to a gash in the bark of the cow tree, sucks the milk

        (as the indian babe drew milk from his father's breast

a man blows a palmwood flute to welcome the ripening palm fruits,

[17]

dons a herondown headdress, avoids bloodshed and the flesh of his patron fish, takes to wife a fat girl with a slender brow, and, to conjure, smokes an armlength cigar

a strip of yellow palm leaf, rolled and folded, with a pendant, a red ornament, sheaths the penis, while the ceramic tanga, in the shape of an arrowhead, a pointed tooth, is magic cover for the vulva

the liquor trough is filled with paiwarrie, the men running a race to it, the winner plunging in, drinking, splashing, bathing in paiwarrie—like the pacific fisherman, immersed

g.

the earth is a great creature, the rivers the bloodvessels, the earth turns one way and another, to warm itself at the sun . . . the first man mated with a gentle doe, and deerlike, generation by generation, the race of indians evolved . . . out of the phallus of the chief came the first maize, from his head, gourds

the spirit of the bird is in his feathers, of the flower in its blossom—a flower, at the fullest bloom, is dangerous, to be avoided

it is death to
sleep under the molle bush

the great serpent, mother of waters, will draw
an indian to his mouth with an inspiration of breath

a floating log, fish
or boa, or the rays of the sun, may invade a woman, bring forth a child deformed . . . the rainbow—shadow of the great waterserpent—will get her with demon

[18]

there is the wild man of the woods, a hairy little creature, strong and wiry, with feet on backwards, who loves to carry off indian women

the freshwater dolphin takes the shape and form, performs the office, of an absent husband

in a jungle full of ghosts, it is wise for a man to make many noises, to establish his vitality

the falling stars are urine, the dew saliva of the stars

h.

cut a piece from the stem of the ayahuasca, beat it in a mortar with water —allow it to steep, and force through a sieve, to separate the woody fibre —to the residue, add water, and drink:

demons in the stem of the plant, the old ones, are seen: jaguar, eagle, anaconda, crocodile—the old ones who went west beyond the mountains, feasted and drank beer, returned as

     fox   llama   puma   the giant blue morpho
     hummingbird   vulture
     uturuncu: the manjaguar
     nosebear   anaconda   dolphin
     otter   treetrunk   heron

i.

in the dance a man holds close to his body a phallus of bast, and with
his hand spreads the seed through house and field

a girl wears the vaginal bone of the freshwaterporpoise, keeps a bushhut
for lovers, and

> the tortoises stumble over each other in the night, clawing the
> sand, digging nests for eggs, laying, crowding, covering and lay-
> ing, breaking the eggs, digging and laying, shoving

> in the morning, when the indian moves among them, the mad
> tortoise still arches her hind leg, clawing, laying

j.

How to make Mosquito Soup.

RECIPE.—Descending the Missouri or Arkansas rivers in North
America, or the Corontyns or Uruguay in South America, run your canoe
ashore in a thick bottom, just at sundown, having filled your tin kettle
about half full of river water, which is very pure and wholesome. Before
landing, however, throw a couple of spoonfuls of salt (or, what is better,
if you have it, half a pound of salt pork) and one of black pepper into
your kettle, and a dozen or so of the small prairie onion (*cop-o-blos*) . . .
   All these things be sure to arrange before you land, as it might be
difficult to arrange them on shore. Also, before being put on shore, if

[20]

you be the cook, you should draw a pair of Indian buckskin leggings over your pantaloons, tying them very tight around the ankles. Leave your hat or cap behind, covering the head with a large silk handkerchief or shawl, passing under the chin, and covering the face as high as the bridge of the nose, and tie it firmly in the back of the neck: then, with a branch of willow boughs in your left hand to protect your eyes (keeping it constantly in motion), whilst your right hand is free to work with, a thick pair of buckskin gloves or mittens on your hands, and your pantaloon pockets turned inside out, your person is tolerably secure from all approach, and you may venture to step ashore but keeping your body and limbs constantly more or less in motion . . .

In these heavy wooded bottoms there is always a plenty of dried mulberry limbs and trees, which gather as quick as possible; they burn free, with a light flame and little or no smoke to frighten the mosquitos away. Set your kettle exactly in the middle of the fire, so that the flame will rise equally all around it, and some twelve or fourteen inches above its rim, which is abundantly high.

The rest of the party, having left you ashore, should then lose no time in paddling into the stream, each one with a bunch of willow-boughs whipping ashore all the insects that are attempting to follow the canoe, and leaving you, the cook, alone to 'walk the kettle', as one alone concentrates the flying cloud better than several.

The cloud beginning to gather in promising quantities around you, you may commence walking at a regular pace, with short steps, around the fire and boiling kettle; and whilst keeping your eyes clear with the willow-boughs in your left hand, if you aim your blows right, a great many may be thus knocked into the kettle that perhaps are too wary to get their wings burned.

There is no limited time for this operation, nor any end to the arriving multitudes but you must be guided entirely by the apparent quantity, by lifting off the kettle occasionally, when the boiling ceases, and their carcasses rise in a large clotted mass on the surface, which with a large spoon you should throw off, as the *fat* is all extracted from them, and their bodies should give way to a fresh supply, in order to obtain the requisite richness of the soup.

[21]

If you observe occasionally a gallinipper or a mosquito hawk falling in, which is very apt to be the case, where they are so confusedly grouped together, all the better, for they are always gorged with a fresh supply of these insects; and if in the desperate struggle any part of your dress should have given way, and the mosquitos should have succeeded through the breach in getting a few ounces of your blood, no matter—never mind it; it will add to the richness of the soup.

The boiling operation being finished, and the canoe called ashore, the kettle should be handled as quickly as possible, and taken on board; all hands, as they are armed each with a bunch of willow-boughs, will be able to whip the following swarms ashore as the canoe enters the current, over which they never venture to fly more than a few rods.

Then, landing on some barren sand-bar which has no vegetation, and consequently is uninhabited by these torments, a comfortable night's rest may be enjoyed; and the soup, when it is sufficiently cooled, and the again collected mass of their light and emptied carcasses floating on the surface are again skimmed off with the spoon, and some hard biscuits crumbled in, your kettle of 'Mosquito Soup' is ready for use.

GEO. CATLIN, Rio Uruguay

k.

the rivers burst the mountains, pour and twine east—canoepaths in the varzeas—to the freshwater inland ocean:

the amazon

freshets at the foot of the andes, october rains in upland bolivia push into the madeira, tapajor, purus, spread over the flood plains, north into the juniperwaters of the negro—these subsiding, the spring rains in

[22]

guiana, venezuela press down, drive into the now sluggish waters to the south:

an annual tide, the serpentriver—amarumayu—rolling and swaying, northward, southward, across the eastward flow

when the plains are in flower, fish swim over the land, the indian lives on mats hung from the crown of the palm, or retreats to his upland hut, where cricket, snake and lizard creep into his thatch, the armadillo, the gran bestia sit by the door, the jaguar stands by, quiet, as the waters rise

padre fritz lived three months in a treetop, grasping fish, plantain and fruit from the waters, fighting off crocodiles

the river undercuts the banks, and the land—a mat of roots and shifting silt—slips away . . . trees crash, the waves beat the opposite shore: back and forth, waves beating from riveredge to riveredge, hour after hour, land and trees crashing, terra cahida, the roar of artillery

bits of land tear loose and float: beds of water hyacinth, mats of brush, of soil, root, plant and tree—rafts for anaconda, alligator, tapir—freshwater floating islands

at the mouth, beyond marajao, the amazonas, clayyellow, filled with timber, weed and moss, turbid, an inland ocean folded northward by equatorial current, ocean river—the amazonas—freshwaters undercutting crumbling banks of salt atlantic—plunges, rolls, upwelling

[23]

THREE

a.

sodomite giant of tumbez, amazon marajao broke pride, converged, and brought forth nudos, altiplano, cordilleras blanca and negra—the mountains called antis

or an ancestorgod, incaic, shaped the ranges with boulders shot from his huaraca—as huanacaure, brother to manco ccapac, later split the hills with a throw

on chimborazo, icecliffs, fed by the jungle trades, project from the peak, westward—tons of ice break away, fall, touch nothing, crash at the glacier's head, the ice shattering, fragments clambering over one another, grinding, rolling, clouds of ice spraying beyond

cinderash from cotopaxi fills the air, blinds alvarado's soldiers—the sky is misted, snow falls

vicuñas idle in the snowbanks, viscachas in the rocks—the llama munches ichu, and moves over the puna

above, the condor's wings are motionless, doorhinged

below the snowline grow the tola, the queñua, the saffron quishuar

the nazca indian comes up from the coast, welcomes the soft wools—alpaca, vicuña—for his loom

for campaigns and conquests, the inca makes maps in relief, little models of the mountains

[24]

b.

near titicaca it is better than a hundred in the sun, near frost in the shade—on illimani, below zero at dawn, above seventy at noon

the indian in ecuador, in a day, brings ice from glacier, chirimoya from jungle, to where apple, peach, pear grow

the fig tree in mala gives fruit on the sierra side in one season, the coastal side in the other

at tequendama the rio de bogotá falls in one leap from cold country to palms

the hummingbird of patagonia flies in the snow

c.

snow and thunder drive across the altiplano, the snowy egret rises, circles

on a glaring, cloudless day the gale drives stones across the ground, cuts hand and face, dries the dead without putrefaction

"Without doubt this is a kinde of cold so piercing that it quencheth the vitall heate, cutting off his influence"

the man on the high peak, the sun blazing on him, looks down on snow-clouds, on lightning cracking over banks of snow

[25]

d.

fireshowers of fallingstars pour on cayamba, in the clear air of copiapo
a planet is seen at noon

at sunrise the mistsea rolls, rises, breaks against grass, snow, rockescarp-
ment, and the sun fires an arm through

a man stands, his head between sun and mistbillows, and the anthelion,
the rainbownimbus shines: the shadow of his head in the mist haloed in
circlets, coronets

setting, the sun drops below cloudwaves, shooting in retreat through
gaps, the world upsidedown, sunlit from below

e.

the heart gives a bruit, a sawlike sound—the red marrow is abundant,
active—the little indians' cheeks are plumcolored, blue in the red,
cyanotic

the problem being, at high altitude, ventilation

> the indian draws in breath and blows on the quena . . . at night
> he draws his knees to his chin, to sleep, the thighs conserving
> vital heat

"the quality of the ayre cutteth off man's life"

[26]

in some, a depression, a lack of will

in others, *surumpe*: the sun breaks through snowclouds, with wind and dry air pierces the eyes—the indian sits by the roadside, shrieking, eyes in flames, lids bleeding, swollen, stuck fast—snowblind

or *soroche*: the head swims, throbs, the veins turgid—breath comes short, the heart a drumbeat—hands and feet chilled, lips and eyelids swollen, bleeding

jose de acosta "was surprised with such pangs of straining and casting as I thought to cast vp my soul too: for having cast vp meate, fleugme, and choller, both yellow and greene, in the end I cast vp blood, with the straining of my stomacke"

the will oppressed, the urge to drown, or fornicate

> Rx: *surumpe*: fresh bloody flesh of vicuña, laid on the eyes
>
> *soroche*: unguent of tallow, garlic and wild marjoram on the forehead . . . infusion of coca . . . copulation

[27]

FOUR

a.

in the eastandean foothills, fossil lacustrine limpets are found, and in the upland, above timberline, pliocene marine deposits—testaceous remains . . . at the summit of the andean arch, sub-tropical fossil floras

walled in to the east, the continent enclosed vast mediterraneans: the amazon sea, mojos lake, the sea of the pampas

rain fell over the old mountains, preandean, and over the low altiplano . . . the clouds refilled from titicaca, and the deserts of gran peru flushed green

but the continent thrust to the west, against basement complex rocks, precambrian—a resistent mass—and the young andes uparched—epeirogenic—overlying, truncating the old mountain roots

b.

a man is anxious, restless, a pressure on the breast—the frame shudders, limbs tremble

[28]

seabirds fly inland to the cordillera, dogs disappear, vicuñas descend
from the mountains, mingle in the streets with indians

the sound is lowpitch, between hearing and feeling, as, remote thunder,
a groan and rattle, the crepitation of burning wood—the earth a thin-
shell cavern, thumping

a man's footing is oscillatory, fluid: the desert curls, sand-columns rising,
whirling, the mountain peaks wave like reeds

the river at arequipa turned black and sulphurous
                                        near chillan the earth
bubbled and burst, hot, fetid waters swelled out
                                  not far from arica a num-
ber of skeletons, legs flexed on the pelvis, were heaved from the ground
steam issued from pasagua bay, itself a crater
                                        the ocean bubbled, smoke
and bursts of flame erupting
                            at callao the pacific withdrew from the shore,
paused, and, foam-capped, smooth as milk, rolled inland

lava welled out of cotopaxi, shoved blocks of ice and snow before it,
caused floods in latacunga (indians thought the crater yielded seawater
and fish

ashclouds rose, the sun turned green, the sky verdigris, copper, bloodred,
brass

at riobamba, below sangai, the land reshaped, mountains sprouted, rivers shifted, disappeared
                        cacha vanished
                                    near cuzco rivers sprang in dry
gullies
            a ridge thrust across the rio seco
                                    the shellmarked coast lifted, up-
arching from the ocean, and held

[29]

old stream beds and valleys—babes to the andean canyons—are crossed, buried beneath vulcanism, intrusive granite

the cordillera blanca, uparching, cuts the trades, jungle rains become ice sheets, and coastal gran peru, green, dries to a desert

toxodons, camelidae vanish in the puna beds

> hot sun follows the snow, the hills groan, rocks split, flakes of stone and soil fall down the slopes

> the limestones are pitted, the porphyries sculptured—skullshape granites onionpeel, quartzite erodes

> young andes reshape rock wastes, reform the stream flows

> and the indian intrudes

FIVE

a.

at the crux, the area of titicaca:

opposite the golfo del peru, a structural
reentrant in the westward thrust of the continent

crustally unstable, subject to shallow and deepfocus vulcanism, with
thrust faults and overturned folds on the long axis of the lake

titicaca:
caught viselike between the cordilleras

(kjopa-kjahuana is produced by blockfaulting, soto island may
be a horst

dust is washed from the uru, as he sails in his balsa through waterspout-
columns, rising from titicaca
hailstones—chij-chi—whiten the ground,
the june snows cover koati
winds flash in sudden gusts through the straits
of tiquina and yampupata
bluewinged teal, black diver, white and black
gull feed in the waters, snipe skim the beach, white crane stalk the lake-
edge shallows
the wind throws a thicketful of parrots into the air, herons
issue from the yellow waterreed
near the lake, a stunted olive, wild straw-
berry and cabbage grow

[31]

the andes thrust up, passed an arm around pacific waters, cupping them from the ocean—when bottoms in the shallows are stirred, seashells foam to the surface: early titicaca, an inland ocean, fed by glaciermelt and rains from the yungas, grew and spread

> the world was dark, and the sun, flameshape, burst from wildcat rock

at tihuanacu, on the south shore, titicacatihuanacu man, lacustrine, andeanocean man, intruded

b.

at the centre, willka, the sun: rising over snowy cordillera, warming the high plain, the sunvicuña, sunllama, early american camel, sunanimal: wariwillka

world, the centre of the universe, tihuanacu, the centre of the world— at tihuanacu, taypicala: taipiri, centre, and ccala, worked stone: a block of andesite, worked by man—wariwillkastone, the sunstone:

> faced full front, he stands on a socle, at the summit of the hollow cavern, earth

> > (the earth is a stepped pedestal, terraced: ocean to desert to mountain to high plain to mountain to jungle— earth salient, reentrant—accute and obtuse

> and within, the inner earth, the moonhouse: the puma, enclosed —with longnecked condor, and wariwillka, upreaching—in the cavern, earth

[32]

at the extreme of the sign—the ends of the earth—wari-
willkas, the eyes winged (impregnating), head crowned,
condorfeathered

and above, at the summit of the socle, the springequinox, wariwillka, septembersun

the head is crowned, the supreme crown: star signs and
sunanimal heads (the necks jointed, moving)—condorfeathered puma at the brow, faced full front

around the full face, as a fillet, signs of earthsteps, with skies
superimposed

the face human, a full nose, sight in full flight from the
phalliceyes, winged, sunanimalcrowned

from the jaw, five stars (flight of the voice), and on the chest,
full centre, a birdtailed puma (the body in motion) over the sun,
with condors bordering, upreaching

across shoulders, condors and sunsigns, and at the belt,
sunanimals, with pumaheads, trophies, suspended

warwillkas, earth and sky on the arms—from the elbow, a trophy
head faced full front: the sunthief, killed at the solstice

in the hands, sceptres, top and bottom condor crowned,
the female and the crested condormayku

this—the sunfigure—springsun at the year's beginning—the indian
worked in andesite

and beneath, spreading at its feet, carved a frieze, a meander,
with the year's other parts, the months solstice to solstice

the world—tihuanacu—guarded from suntheft—june
and december—the northern and southern ends of the
earth—by a mighty, crested condor mayku

[33]

c.

the blocks quarried in the north, floated on rafts of totora reed, across titicaca

the carving: conflation of llama, puma, fish, cougar, condor
earth, sun,
moon, sky
of the stepsign, stepsign with volute
chachapuma, pachamama

the sunfigure, rafted and carved—mounted, by andean man, on the platform of kalasasaya

at akapana, the fortress: stone angles salient and reentrant, for defense—
as at kalasasaya, salient and reentrant stone repelled ignorance, conserved knowledge: the southern cross, solstice and equinox, distribution of the seasons

in the centre of the earth, a puma, nibbling the moon—from full to crescent

and letting it grow again

and a giant wariwillka—sunanimal—stamping, shaking

SIALIA

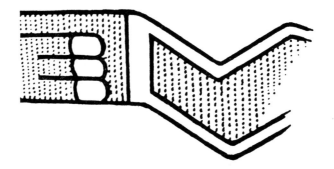

a.

d'Étroit,
as sieur de la mothe cadillac
saw it:

the narrows would
control the lakes . . .

b.

Preliminary Remarks:

> *RULE.*—Before attempting to read a lesson, the learner should
> make himself fully acquainted with the subject, as treated of in
> that lesson, and endeavor to make his own, the feelings and sen-
> timents of the writer.

Articulation:

> *RULE I.*—Avoid the omission or improper sound of unaccented
> vowels, whether they form a syllable or part of a syllable . . .

> *RULE II.*—Guard particularly against the omission, or the
> feeble sound of the terminating consonant.

> *RULE III.*—Avoid uniting into one word, syllables which be-
> long to different words.

[37]

Tones:

> *RULE I.*—The reader or speaker should choose that pitch, on which he can feel himself most at ease, and above and below which he may have the most room for variation.

> *RULE II.*—The tones of the voice should always correspond with the nature of the subject.

Inflections:

> *RULE I.*—The falling inflection is generally proper, wherever the sense is complete . . .

> *RULE II.*—Language which demands strong emphasis, generally requires the falling inflection.

> *RULE III.*—Questions, which *cannot* be answered by *yes* or *no*, together with their answers, generally require the falling inflection . . .

> *RULE IV.*—Where a pause is rendered proper by the meaning, and the sense is incomplete, the rising inflection is generally required . . .

> *RULE V.*—Questions which *may* be answered by *yes* or *no*, generally require the *rising*, and their answers the *falling* inflection . . .

> *RULE VI.*—The different members of a sentence expressing comparison, or contrast, or negation and affirmation, or where the parts are united by or used disjunctively, require different inflections: generally the *rising* inflection in the *first* member, and the *falling* inflection in the *second* member. This order is, however, sometimes inverted.

McGuffey's
Newly Revised
Eclectic Fourth Reader

c.

east of the appalachian barrier the pioneer brought out jebediah morse's geography, and studied: the fertility of michigan, the fruit and wild grapes, the freshwater lakes

he headed west, over corduroy and gumbo, beneath treetops shaken by the wind as an ocean surface, agitated

the man moved into the forest with an axe, to fight it, drive it back

as the distance grew—from albany, new york, philadelphia—words turned to whispers, whispers to silence—he read an old newspaper, and, wordless, held with cool ardor to his axe: immersed and virgin in the timber

out of dearbornville he felled logs for a house, and men came to help raise them—black ash were cut and peeled, the bark laid on for a roof

a green black oak was felled, the man sawed off bolts, rived out shakes with a froe, laid them up with clay, for a chimney

at night he got a backlog in—rolling it on sticks, moving chairs and table aside, crowding it in place, over the clay hearth—against it he set michigan andirons: bolts of green wood—and laid the foresticks on

late, as the coals glowed, a boy could stand on the hearth, look through the flue at michigan constellations

a clearing was made, trees ringed or felled

the axe driven into rooty dirt, corn seed dropped in the cleft, the axe driven close to close the cleft

[39]

pontiacers—flies the size of young hummingbirds—swarmed in the brush, and the blue racer outraced the pioneer

the first crop—wheat or corn—fought in the clearing with stumps, trunks, shoots, weeds and vines

one william ford—who had known tenantry in ireland—cleared ninety acres, with patches of timber, called it Springwells Township Farm

> july 30 1863, his wife mary gave birth to a first son: the boy henry

d.

it was like jefferson: to play roughly at the fiddle, and to lighten—or en-lighten!—the burden

out of springwells—or skylighted monticello—the rustic, giving play to gyrations, to wheels

> (young jefferson pushed through the snows with his bride to reach the little cottage off the main house
>
> and years later, stood on the monticello porch watching progress at the university, through a telescope

jefferson: backeast, east of appalachia, but hugging the mountains, push-ing—the modern mind spilling over, to all louisiana

and later, northward, to michigan

"Mr. Ford still believes it is early morning in America . . ."

[40]

father took the little boy by the hand to show him a song sparrow nest:
by the big oak, twenty rods east of home and birthplace, and the boy heard
the bird sing

he took walks alone in the ten eyck estate, or in the virgin tracts east of
the rouge

in winter, skated down roulo creek to the rouge, down the rouge to the
detroit, and up to woodward avenue

in summer, bathed in the rouge, south of michigan avenue: dared to
swim far out, to pick water lilies

or, saturdays, hitched the team, with father and brother, hauled hay,
grain and wood, apples, potatoes, to the haymarket

       (which is now a greensward, a stadium

          (for lions and tigers

f.

they asked the grown man, years later, the lawyer at the chicago tribune
libel trial, mr. ford, he said, what was the united states originally? and
henry unclasped a jackknife, honed it on the leather of his shoe, took his
own good time and replied, without looking up,

land, I guess

[41]

g.

they asked him, elsewhere, what he would do if he were to take charge
of american farms

      tear down all the fences, he said.

      but what about animals overrunning your crops?

      there wouldn't be any animals, he replied. there is no reason why
any farmer should have horses. tractors are better and cost much less.
better milk can be and has been made out of vegetable products than
any cow can give. the cattle that we need for food and sheep that we need
for wool should be raised on great ranges in the west . . .

he built a chemurgical workship, hired greenhorns with no notions,
poured cabbages, carrots, onions, melons into the caldrons . . . word
came that before long we should grow most of an automobile, perhaps
grow a complete car of wheat

stacks of cornstalks and sunflowers went into the hoppers

h.

january 12, 1904—ford, with clara and edsel, and spider huff, drove
northeast to anchor bay, lake st. clair

scraped snow from the ice, spread cinders

turned loose the model b, an overpriced lemon (the particular car being

barney oldfield's 999), ford at the wheel and spider blowing in the tank
to keep the gas feeding, made the measured mile—the car leaping, skid-
ding over ice, fissures, cinders—in 39 seconds plus

i.

"Everything is in flux, and was meant to be. Life flows."

there was this thing he had about *water*: the love of old water-powered
mills, the fixing of factories and assembly plants by rivers, for power,
the placing of freight on ships rather than RRs

he hated history: "The water that is up the river, and the water now going
over the wheel, are of more importance to youngsters than water that
already has gone out to sea."

books "mussed up his mind" and "Reading can become a dope habit . . .
Booksickness is a modern ailment."

threw out paperwork, recordkeeping, statistics—the *statics* (as ole diz
calls 'em)

had no fixed corporate structure, no titles (the men in his research labs
had desks but no chairs)—preferred, instead, a *fluid* structure, execu-
tives with no defined responsibilities, competing, warring with one another, the organization kinetic, life and factory an assembly line, moving,
an amazon, mainflow and affluents

"Life . . . is not a location but a journey"

[43]

"Life is a going concern"

"The most beautiful things in the world are those from which all excess weight has been eliminated"

j.

june 1 1909—start of a crosscountry race, new york to puget sound:

>(the checking stations: new york — poughkeepsie — albany — syracuse — rochester — buffalo — erie — cleveland — toledo — south bend — chicago — bloomington — st. louis — centralia — kansas city — manhattan — ellsworth — oakley — denver — cheyenne — rock river — wamsutter — granger — pocotello — bliss — boise — walla walla — pendleton — seattle

>the pathfinder car couldn't make it, quit in idaho—another, starting in seattle, found snow, snoqualmie pass, seventeen feet

new york city, president taft pushed a gold key, the mayor fired a gold revolver, five cars started: an acme, a shawmut, an itala and two fords

at cleveland, the summer rains: the toledo run made in "mud in bunches . . . gummy, clayey, clinging mud"

st. louis west, rain and hail, hensegg metaldenting hailstones, cloudbursts, beside which a michigan downpour was but the "falling of the dew"

gumbo and quagmire, mud to the axles, swollen streams, with quicksands,

[44]

to be forded, driver and mechanic tearing down old pigpens, running on the planks

wagonroads, mule trails, or no trail at all, misguided guides in the desert

east of topeka, ford #2 slid off a bank into a stream—the two men re-moved the damaged axle, carried it 3 miles to a blacksmith, got repairs, carried 3 miles back, installed, and resumed

crossed the river platte on the ties of a RR bridge

west of cheyenne, driver and mechanics held tight, so not to be thrown, as the fords climbed

snoqualmie pass: #1 smashed a rock, and the crew rebuilt the motor at the continental divide
                        #2 skimmed over the frozen surface of snow, sank as the sun warmed, was dug out by a section gang
                                            and came on to puget,
the winner!

            carrying, in its front tires, original air from new york city

k.

Processes On The Crank Box:

        Apply drop-forging half ring to rear end, drill three pin holes,
                put in pins.
        Rivet pins both ends.
        Seat and drill front vertical wall for four rivets.

[45]

Burr up rivet ends to retain rivets.

Head front-wall rivets, by hand.

On anvil with hand-hammer and 'staking' tool, stake front wall to fill.

On surface plate, gauge and with hand-hammer bring job to overall length.

Apply globe seat for front-axle globe-end radius-fork.

Drill for two rivets, to fix globe-bracket position.

In press, rivet ends of globe-bracket.

First braze; rear-end reinforce, made in four-fire, hand-revolved brazing-furnace.

Braze globe-seat bracket. Vertical flames both upward and downward.

On emory wheel, polish arm-seats.

Face end of rear annular collar flush with crank-box shell end.

Back to big press line, and in final die straighten up the job, far as completed.

> *I asked my mother for fifty cents*
> *To see the elephant jump the fence.*
> *He jumped so high*
> *He reached the sky*
> *And never came back till the Fourth of July.*

Re-rivet front-wall rivets, stretched by preceding operation.

Bring walls to length with press surface-jig.

Grind flat over walls at ends.

Pierce two holes for drain-cock flange; also, same operation, seat and close in the drain-cock seat ready for tapping.

Rivet splash-plate.

On driller, half-globe ream front axle radius-ball seat.

> *Mary had a little lamb*
> *Its fleece was black as tar.*
> *And everywhere that Mary went*
> *They thought it was a b-a-a-r.*

Drill thirty-one holes, Bausch Machine Company's driller.

Burr thirty-one drilled holes.

Punch three rivet holes in each arm-seat.

Drill fourteen transmission cover holes.

Burr fourteen drilled holes.

Punch three holes in front and bottom.

Ream front wall for starting-crank sleeve seat.

Punch overflow screw-seat-bush holes.

Fix front-end malleable-iron casting trunnion in place with two rivets.

Drill six more trunnion rivet holes.

Hand-rivet six rivets in trunnion.

Close in the two overflow-plug bushes, to be tapped to take the overflow screws. These screws are at different levels, to show maximum and minimum oil plash-pool depths in crank-box-fly-wheel-housing depression.

Press-rivet six rivets in end trunnion shell.

Turn crank-box shell projections down over trunnion shell, with hand-hammer.

Braze trunnion shell to crank-box shell, in four-hole, hand-revolved brazing furnace.

On a large cast-iron jig, with legs and clamp and spotting pins, gauge and straighten the trunnion.

Drill trunnion hole.

With angle plate on face-plate and lathe and back-rest fixture, turn trunnion.

> *I eat my peas with honey,*
> *I've done it all my life.*
> *It makes the peas taste funny,*
> *But it keeps them on my knife.*

With crank-box clamped to lathe-saddle spotting-fixture, bore and face rear-end brazed-in drop-forging annular collar.

Drill and tap screw holes in rear-end collar.

Place the two pressed-steel hangers by which crank-box is held to
chassis frame, drill for and insert three pins, and rivet pin
ends, to hold hangers to crank-box shell.

Braze crank-box hangers to crank-box shell, four fires in a bank,
with swinging flames on top, stationary flames below.

By hand, with big file end, scrape and clean inside of crank-box
shell.

By hand, finish-tap rear-collar screw holes.

Place transmission covers, with gaskets applied to covers; place
horse-shoe reinforces inside of crank-box, and put in fourteen transmission cover screws, through covers, through
gaskets, through crank-box shell, and turn screws down
hard; screws threaded into the two horse-shoe reinforces.

Oats, peas, beans and barley grows,
Oats, peas, beans and barley grows,
How, you nor I nor nobody knows,
Oats, peas, beans and barley grows.

In large fixture, with gauge and hand-hammer, bring the crank-
box hangers to place.

Lay crank-box, flat side down, on large surface plate, and with
hand-hammer make the crank-box top flange lie down
on the surface plate, all the way around.

Entry, kentry, cutry, corn,
Apple seed and apple thorn.
Wire, brier, limber lock,
Three geese in a flock.
One flew east, one flew west,
One flew over the cuckoo's nest.
O-U-T spells out goes she.

In a large fixture, with clamps, with hand-hammer, bring the
hanger holes to slide on fixture pins.

[48]

Tap globe-seat cap holes for cap retention.

Tap drain screw seat.

Tap the two overflow screw seats.

Fill overflow screw seats with temporary brass screws, screwdriver cuts, to close holes for gasoline leak tests.

Tap two holes in rear-end annular collar, and two holes in front vertical wall.

Heat front side of front wall, and clean wall and box wall seat with muriatic acid, to clean the surfaces for soft-soldering.

With tinning fluid and hand soldering-copper, soft-solder front wall in place to the crank-box shell inside.

With hand copper, fill joint with soft-solder and also fill top joint between box wall and the front wall, if joint is open on top side.

With hand-file end clean off surplus solder.

> *Hacker, packer, soda cracker,*
> *Hacker, packer too.*
> *Hacker, packer, soda cracker,*
> *Out goes you.*

Place drain screw and turn it down hard.

Press the hand starting-crank bushing into place in center of trunnion.

Place crank-box, open side up, in gasoline vat and see if any gasoline leaks into the box at any point.

> *Onery, uery, ickory Ann,*
> *Filisy, folasy, Nicholas John*
> *Queever, quaver, English neighbor,*
> *Stinkem, stankem, B-bo-buck.*

Final. Dip in air-drying japan vat, to japan outside of crank-box.

Quaker, Quaker, how is thee?
Very well, I thank thee.
How's thy neighbor next to thee?
I don't know, but I'll go see.

1.

among maples, where the ann arbor trail crosses the rouge, stood nankin,
the old grist mill restored, producing dies and engravings for fords—
the neighboring farmers gained winter employment in the mill, sent
their children to the red brick schoolhouse

The rural production centre, ideal community:

jefferson at monticello, ripley at brook farm, ford at nankin
                                                                  oneida,
new harmony, joseph smith and elbert hubbard
                                        hedgerow theatre, black
mountain college; community in the arts
                                mack avenue, highland park:
for the deserving worker, the $5 day
                        blithedale: the plant on the river
rouge

m.

on a picnic with edison, ford ran, jumped, yelled and hollered, chopped
logs, climbed trees

        he and edison once held a kicking contest, new york
hotel: it was edison who won, bringing down the chandelier

                again, ford
disappeared on board a train, returned later covered with soot: he had
climbed the coalcar, hobnobbed with the engineer, ran the locomotive

often he hopped in and out of his office by way of the windows

n.

the oscar II, the peace ship—her hull glistening in the low winter sun—
slipped into the hudson currents

        I saw a little fordship
        go chugging out to sea . . .

in the atlantic, ford, taking his brisk michigan morning walk, was
drenched by a wave—he caught cold and retired to his cabin

(the newsmen made up their own stories, from the ship's bar)

once he snuck out, went below, was for a moment happy, inspecting
machine shop and engine room

[51]

the ship docked in norway, ford was sick and grim—the winter sun set early

dean marquis—working for the family to persuade ford to give it up—put him in a gloomy room, heavily curtained, with northern exposure—and locked the door

it was christiana!

ford passed hours alone, working—alone—for peace

o.

the sense of touch, the *real* thing

> (when bill durant, forming general motors, tried to buy out ford, ole hank said, all right, but gold on the table!

> (a money he could touch

he disliked blue prints, worked from models

"I wouldn't give five cents for all the art in the world" and once spent time hanging around artist's studios trying to find out what it was, the intangible

"History is more or less bunk" but there were wayside inn and greenfield village, a *real* history

touch sense, the genius of touch:

[52]

they decide to contract for a part of the car, say a distributor head—the samples come in, maybe 30 of them, the engineers spend days studying, take them apart, work them over, figure out which is the best

all 30 are spread on a table and ford comes in, squints at them, picks one up here and there—after a couple of minutes says, *that one*

and so it is

and some wag brought him an alien washer, asked where it belonged on a model t—he grasped it and threw it out the window, knew by the touch that it didn't

william carlos williams: ideas only in things . . . *the animism of the indian!*

the hand at work, in touch—the mind liberated, made meditative

or ford's fellowmiddlewesterners, dreiser and anderson, groaning to make their art *real*, to put the *self* on the page—man and art indistinguishable

the man and the thing made—ford & ford—one

p.

when asked the secret of his life, he replied that he was leonardo da vinci, reincarnate

"What we call death doesn't end all for us, by any means"

[53]

"When the automobile was new, and one of them came down the road, a chicken would run straight for home—and usually get killed. But today when a car comes along, a chicken will run for the nearest side of the road. That chicken has been hit in the ass in a previous life."

His own first car was only part of an accumulated experience, inherited at birth

(the transmission was planetary)

and three worlds from now the ford would be a better car than ever

for the nation, a car—a carnation!
not an inca, but re-inca—in car!

reincarnation!

q.

little harry bennett came out of the navy, to run the show at the rouge

hired cons, thugs, pluguglies—on the side raised beef, chows, horses, played the sax, thought *moby-dick* the greatest book ever written

when he rode with ford, he was armed—the chauffer had a gat under each arm, and there were magnum revolvers in a holster built into the car

in his office he shot target practice with goldplated revolver

harry bennett was director of personnel

[54]

march 7 '32—an icy day—a crowd—fordjobless, commies, hang-
erson—gathered in detroit, and marched to the rouge . . . at the
city line—baby creek park—the dearborn cops pumped tear gas
shells: the mob got mad, hurled rocks, fought through, unarmed,
to miller road, the overpass at gate 3:

bennett's thugs, inside the gate, turned firehose and firearm on
the hunger marchers, wounding, killing: the battle of the rouge

      and later, ford men tore up the soybean acres, planted
      them in cement for bombers, at willow run

r.

milk is poisonous, and salt is good for the hair

"I've got no use for a motor that has more spark plugs than a cow has
teats"

s.

at fair lane, virgin oaks, willows, elms stood among the second growth

handmade bricks from coon ten eyck's tavern were built into the fireplace

[55]

the bobolinks came back to dearborn every year on april 2 . . . there were five hundred bird houses at fair lane, the largest, the martin house, held seventy-six apartments—the wren boxes hung from strips of spring steel, to discourage sparrows—pheasants and quail were hatched, incubated, and through the winter wire baskets of food hung from the trees, and the bird baths were electrically heated

corn was grown, left standing for the squirrels, and little stacks of rails and hay were built to house the rabbits

(but the english birds imported—hammer, chaffinch, twit, bull-finch, thrush, linnet, lark—scattered and vanished in the michigan plain, and the doves at greenfield fell prey to michigan hawks

(the rabbits flourished, overran fair lane, destroyed the orchards, he had his men tear down their homes, shoot them as pests

(as, the workers: five-dollar-day to hunger march

(and the heated bird baths failed to break the cycle of migration

ford took a daily walk, chinning himself on lowhanging limbs, and ending at a trot, or a sprint through the cornstalks

entering the door at fairlane, he stood in the hall and whistled for clara . . . they sat on the sunporch and watched birds, binoculars and audubon in hand . . . at night she read aloud to him from bambi and the yearling, and they listened to lum and abner

or he skated alone on the frozen rouge, by moonlight

at the engineering lab in dearborn he maintained musicians: dulcimer, cymbalo, violin and sousaphone . . . the craneway was removed, the machines pushed back: henry and the motormen folk-danced

he named his yacht *sialia*—indian for bluebird—but on board he was

[56]

restless: as they locked through a canal, he vaulted a rail, and footed the distance

"The stars are so bright in Florida, we saw many that cannot be seen here in Dearborn"

sailing the caribean, he would spot a lonely beach: a launch would set him ashore, with clara, and the *sialia* would stand offshore, while the couple rested, or hunted seashells in the sand

t.

"The Rouge is so big that it is no fun any more"

after the old french landrich of detroit came the younger lumberrich, and after them the still younger motorrich—and with all of these ford mixed not at all

he called on grandpa mellie dunham for a fiddletune, and skipped—alone, solemn—through the steps of a waltz

or ambled in the late evening to the stephen foster cottage, greenfield village, and—hunched at the organ—picked with one finger at *the old folks at home*

> (the manager of fordlandia, the rubber plantation on the amazon, came from detroit, and at christmas time he had in his jungle home a christmas tree!

at dearborn, april 7 1947—five days after the arrival of the bobolinks—a rain and windstorm raged, the power failed—the little suwanee, fed

[57]

over a wheel by waters of the detroit river, overflowed in greenfield village, and the sidewheeler foundered . . . up the rouge at fair lane—by the light of oil lamps—ford's own motor came to a halt

in a cardboard box in his private experimental lab, they found a test tube, tightly sealed and neatly labeled:

"Edison's last breath."

SALT, GARLIC & COITION

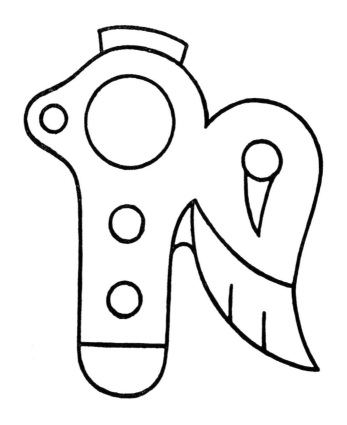

ONE

a.

" . . . knobby joints and a somewhat zigzag stalk, hairy leaf sheathes and stiffish leaves, purplish color in all or several parts of the plant, coarse root system, ears of pyramidal shape (markedly tapering and having a heavy butt), soft, brittle cobs and long glumes, irregularly rowed seeds, and crest tassels."

> " . . . as bygge as a mannes arme in the brawne: The graynes whereof are sette in a marvelous order, and are in fourme somewhat lyke a pease. While they be soure and unripe, they are white: but when they are ripe they be very black. When they are broken, they be whyter than snoww. This kynde of grayne, they call *Maizium*."

out of the montaña, west of the clogged rainforest, but climbing out of it, a typical amazonian plant, with "pendulous leaves, colored foliage, long aerial roots, a cauliflorous inflorescence, small flowers with conspicuous coloring, and a tendency toward the seperation of the sexes in the flowers."

maize moved under the hand of the indian, and the podded hawksbill seeds became naked

marched north, the culturehero!—maize and indian, exfoliating, spreading

[61]

crossed the isthmus and in mexico became tripsicoid: " . . . slender, cane-like growth, elastic and little subject to breaking or lodging, often of bright green color; cylindrical ears; dense woody cobs and short glumes; seeds in straight rows; widely branching tassels; and free tillering."

flooded north and east: navajo and cherokee

the indian putting the plant to use in every growth stage: leaf, blossom, immature and fullgrown fruit—his garden in the field

b.

on the rainless coast of peru the indian grew maize with fishheads and dew, fattened the ground with guano

in the mountains he straightened the rio urubamba—a snake thrashing between valleyedges—contained it within walls, filled soil over loose rock, replaced full stretches of earth, reshaped, regraded the valley

stepped the slopes with terraces, filled with jungle earth, directed glacial water

and, with potatoes, drove glaciers up the ridges

on the steep slopes, he held with one hand and worked the ground with the other—staked the squashes, so they would not roll off

handplowed in crisscross, to hold the steepfalling rains

built cities on hills and hummocks, to save the fat bottoms for cultivation

TWO

a.

the inca drove a wedge between the men drugged—coast indians addicted
to the hills and hummocks, the fat bottoms, the buttocks of their own:
the sodomites

cut off the moche waters to chan-chan, brought the gran chimu to his
knees

took virgins to himself, burned and buried alive those who drove the fish
into unproductive flesh, and

with lusty indians, built an empire to the borders of the condor's range,
panandean

b.

in peru, when the palta ripens, the men and girls fast, abstain from salt,
garlic & coition, for five days . . . they gather in the fruitgardens, nude,
and hold a footrace: as each man reaches a girl, he plants and ripens her,
on the spot

[63]

(intercourse must always occur outdoors, in the cultivated fields—the indoor child will be blind or lazy

between the dying and new moons, the indian goes to his wife, and for nine months, as each month turns new, he goes to her again, engendering the child by degrees, man and moon enlarging it, bringing it full

c.

andean man played the mansize syrinx, drum, tambor and cowhorn—deerbone fife, deerskull whistle, quena, conchshell and bullhorn—a tibia flute (from an enemy), a fivehole flute, a fifteenfoot bamboo horn—and at huantar, set flutes in rockclefts in the mountain, for the updrafts to make music

he spoke quechua: quehuasca, twisted straw—the language aglutinate, polysynthetic, the meanings twisted together—woven to the root, the actionword—or joined, as at machu picchu, stone by stone: meanings so precise that, though without mortar, not a knifeblade may pass between them

his wife twisted vicuña with viscacha and bat wool, spun it clockwise—she gained a carmine dye from the cochineal, used urine as a mordant, and wove three hundred threads to the inch

d.

in the valley of yucay—from pissac to ollantaytampu—the inca might listen to chiuiuiuñichi—air whistling among the leaves of trees—or the songbirds, the doves and pigeons, the tuya, ccenti, checollo, the golden-breasted quitu

he might be misqui-tullu—a sweetbone, lazy fellow—and bathe in mingled hot and cold spring waters, in freestone baths

he wore a mantle of batfur from tumbez, or a garment composed of thousands of the tiny goldgreen feather from the hummingbird's breast

he would dine in the morning, and spend the day drinking (the inca huana ccapac could outdrink his captains, three to one) . . . in the evening, a light supper

his gardens gave chirimoya, palta and lucma, the white maize of yucay, wild cherries from andahuaylas

the cherry tomato grew wild in urubamba

e.

LLANTO

flûte   ♩=96   calme   Cusco (Perou)

HUK URPICATAM UYWAKARKANI

Jauja (Perou)

BAILE DE LOS DANZANTES

Vallée du Chanchamayo (Perou)

KASWA

PASTORALE

lima (Perou)

f.

the inca tupac amaru—his sunvirgins—and a few effeminate males,
were the last to live at machu picchu—a refuge past pizarro

in the air, the blackheaded grosbeak, a sparrow and finch, the gray dove,
the brown robin

bear and deer on the ground—bushmaster and coral

water came from springs on the mountainside, carried by stone into and
through the city: pool, drain, stone, fountain, to pool

       (but in the dry season it must be hauled from the urubam-
       ba two thousand feet below, or from springs miles away

[71]

D'ÉTROIT

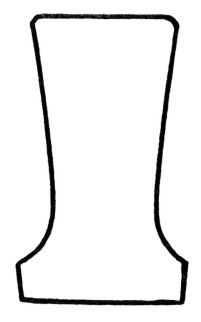

when I go out to gloucester to see charles olson everything works out fine
the east wind the april fog rolling in off the harbor 28 fort square cozy
charles just out of bed rolling out over dinner a rich meal and he drives
me back to the station I make the 8:12 with time to spare due north station 9:19 35 minutes to the airport and another half hour to flight time
the stations click off on schedule until we back out of the salem station
a mile or so and sit for half an hour just the margin I needed to make my
connection we get rolling again and take our time when I get to north
station I rush to the phone call the airline find the plane is delayed 20
minutes and I just might make it I roar to a taxi and bribe the driver heavy
to make time through sumner tunnel and out to east boston at the reservation desk I find the flight is now delayed indefinitely they have no
planes everything coming in late account of the weather I can't possibly
make my connection at idlewild new york for the flight to detroit I'm
about to give up go back to boston get a hotel or take the sleeper when
they announce an earlier flight also delayed just now leaving for new
york I beat my way back to the desk make them hold the flight while I buy
a ticket rush out the gate cross the pavement through driving april rain
board the plane surrender ticket to stewardess door slams motors rev
we cruise to runway gun the sons of bitches and we're aloft

comes now above the cloud layer over the intercom the electronic voice
of the stewardess welcome aboard eastern flight number such-and-such
your hostess miss so-and-so this flight for la guardia field new york and
I think oh great oh great for la guardia and my flight is out of idlewild
across long island with an hour and fifteen minutes to contemplate this
we settle in still raining at la guardia I rush to the reservation desk present my problem plane leaving idlewild for detroit in half an hour I can't
get there and he says yes you can't get there and I look at him and he
looks at me and then he goes to an inner office calls a number to idlewild
comes back out beaming you're in like a bird northwestern flight number
such-and-such idlewild to detroit also delayed by weather yes by taxi four
bucks I can make it

pleasant ride groundborne la guardia to idlewild discuss with driver

[75]

problems of manhattan hack stuck late at night on the island only thing
to do is work the airports hope for a fare back to the city and here I've
crossed him up but at least a fare maybe now he'll be lucky

wild it is but not idle and my flight is further delayed nothing to do for a
couple of hours but find the men's room closed for cleaning sit and contemplate the crowds the dirt the noise and think this I could do at one
third the cost in any united states bus station like everyone else I've been
took and study spanish from the bilingual eastern and national plane an-
nouncements for san juan puerto rico es la ultima llamada

3:10 a.m. airborne for detroit, rain, fog, heavy wind, the plane, cargo
with a few passengers, rocked. I manage to sleep a little

around 5:30, circle into detroit metropolitan airport and land still raining
and blowing hard emerge under the flat steel dawn and cross to the huge
modern terminal building miraculously vacant claim my baggage and
catch a grayhound to the city

> detroit
> a city   no city
>   but
>   only the suburbs of its
>   (as e. e. would say)
>   unself

get a hotel change get breakfast get by phone the routine on the ford
plant rubberneck tour catch an interurban for dearborn walk to the ford
rotunda make the tour

> the ingot afire,
> blasted from the hearth,
> hot in the
> tincovered squaremiles:
>   the rouge

[76]

                    the ingot: lithic, thick
                    —tihuanacu, chavín, san
                    agustín—this it is—mesabi:
                    decanted on a flat car
                    to cool
                    beaten, slapped, chopped, rolled
                    on the line, rolled
                    thin   thin   thin

                    cool & thin
                    a toy
                    for a drug store,
                    a salesroom

back up to dearborn for beer and lunch another bus and another walk to
the edison museum

        henry's agglomeration of all americana, with the crazy machines,
        the old cars, the impact of including the *recent* past (the link),
        the *big* machines, steam plants, etc: the flywheel, 4′ wide, 24′ di-
        ameter, and the avery traction engine, 1916, with the bulldog
        on the front and the words, "teeth talk"

and greenfield village all sentiment all indulgence and here I begin to
give a little

the rain has quit but it is still blowing hard and a few tiny flakes of snow
bite like bugs on my face and the little girl who is to be our guide says in
her funny middle western way there WILL be such and such and you
WILL see so and so and you WILL walk three miles I make it through
henry's birthplace perfectly restored and learn much from this boxing
in of little middle western spaces before frank lloyd wright and into edison's buildings from menlo park with the carloads of original jersey clay
dumped around them the first floor is all right *it's all so very historical*
but on the second in the laboratory where I can look out the windows

across the brick wall and over the highway to the ford experimental grounds I begin to lose track of the nineteenth-century spiel and watch the thunderbirds racing around the experimental track testing testing and here I crap out

the little girl is upset but I tell her I haven't time, I make my way back through the biting weather to the entrance, back on foot to dearborn

> (at the rouge, the overpass on miller road, the blood of them—
> of harry bennett, and those others, the ones who died, the hungry
> white indians who had marched out from the city—the blood of
> them still (so it seems) on the pavement)

and the first drink and think of the second and more and dinner and maybe the gayety burlesque a less official survival in detroit of an older age and a long long night in the madison lenox hotel

7 a.m. two days later a sunday off from willow run the day still gray a delta sixty-seater headed south but a midspring sunday only three or four on board and the stewardess miss so-and-so confused by the mob of us gets the mudtasting coffees mixed the squared fields below still unsprung a gray green and cutting the corner of lake erie over the western islands the freshwater below a graybrown in the smoldering trying-to-emerge early sun that is still only yellow clouds and later to the east tumbling in the low the graylow clouds the land thumping into hills—the hills that barriered jefferson so, to the west, and ford, to the east . . . and west, the flat

SONATAS
IN CAJAMARCA

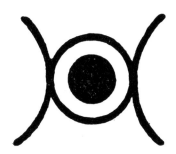

ONE

to the indian, the castilians were

"banished men, with haire on their faces, yea, such as were bred of ye scum of the Sea, without any other Origen or Linage, because the Sea had brought them thither: demaunding also why they wente like Vagabondes wandring the World: it should appeare said they, that you are ydle persons, and have not wherein to imploy your selves, because you abide in no place, to labour and till the ground."

TWO

in manaos, in the rubber boom cobbles from lisbon paved the streets, houses were built of italian tile and marble, with furnishings from france, linen from london, venetian tapestries, mirrors from brussels

grand pianos rotted in the damp, the ladies sent linens to lisbon, to be laundered

tracks of the madeira-mamoré RR were laid on formosan ties, by men from malta, jamaica, wales, barbados, china, martinique, turkey, persia

       (coripuna indians hovered in the jungle

a limeñan hidalgo traveled to iquitos, across the andes and in his own country, by way of panama, transshipping at darien, thence to liverpool, transshipping, again, to belem—and up the amazon

[81]

THREE

> "I have tightened my flute
> with the nerves of a bull
> so that its voice would be clear . . . "

in the jungle colonel fawcett read and reread a wormriddled martin chuz-
zlewit—teddy roosevelt sat on a log, with headnet and gauntlets, and read
"Madame Desbordes-Valmore's lines on the little girl and her pillow,
as dear little verses about a child as ever were written . . . "

in peru, a relay of 40 indians brought a piano over the trail to cajamarca,
and the owner played sonatas

other indians carried pianos, coast to cuzco, and in bolivia, an excep-
tional mule became a pianera: able, singlebacked, to carry a piano over
the andes

> midnineteenth century, the literati in cuzco favored fenimore
> cooper

> the salives indians play well now on the violin-cello

FOUR

a certain limeñan merchant got stuck with a consignment of eyeglasses,
so he went to his amigo, a corregidor in the provinces, and an order was

[82]

issued, that no indian in this corregidor's district should appear at divine
services without spectacles . . . the consignment moved rapidly

the rubberworkers in the jungle traded rubber for tradeguns: the barrels
were made of wire, wound, heated, dipped in solder, and painted—when
fired, the cap snapped, the powder fizzed at length, and the charge left
the muzzle snorting like a wild pig—after 40 or 50 shots, or if too big
a charge were used, the barrel unwound in the indians face, and he
would go to work again, for rubber, and another tradegun

> (the indians in peru at one time were forbidden to cut
> their hair, that they might more easily be dragged by it

> (santa rose indians tied a condor to a bull, exploded fire-
> crackers from the bull's horns

> (in jauja, they went wild, killed white dogs and white
> chickens, scraped whitewash from the walls

FIVE

into the humboldt current the indian smuggles dynamite, spreading it—
the american net—to take fish

> (in rare years, coastal currents and climate are disturbed,
> rain falls, the seabirds go loco, fly inland, feed with cattle
> and swine

when the guano islands were raided, coolies were shipped in by the hun-
dreds from macao, slavedriven to dig guano, to pour the harvest down a

[83]

chute into a ship's hold, where more coolies—lost in the yellow smoke of it, as in a lardfire—balanced the cargo

parts of coolie corpses, vanishing, embalmed in fresh guano, protrude now, make perches

SIX

at tihuanacu, building block and carved stone went into home and church, were blocked and crushed, by the trainload for fill, bridge and culvert, on the RR

the tracks were laid on tihuanacu stone, over ties from oregon

>(in detroit, workers make abstract art from junk, old tail-
>pipes, crankboxes

SEVEN

the dogs at tihuanacu dug up the newburied indian infants, and in chile, the tavernowners bid at auction for the body of an infant: the buyer dressed and painted it, propped open the eyes, set it among candles, and fired off rockets, to announce the wake . . . for three days and nights, business was good

[84]

EIGHT

MANUAL OF INSTRUCTIONS

to catch a condor:

>   hide under a freshly killed animal skin (with meat still adhering)
>   until a condor alights, for the carrion
>
>   grasp him by the legs

to prevent excessive rain:

>   expose a skull
>
>   put a cigarette in its mouth

NINE

a wedding—andeanindian—is an orgy, a

vaginafiesta!

PENSACOLA,
NORTH CAROLINA

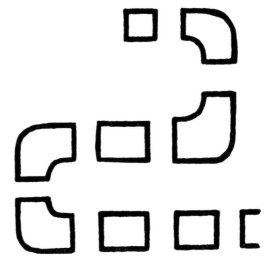

thars this lil ole dirt road, you know, like they had, this lil ole cabin settin up above the road, this ole feller asettin on the porch, and this moll t comes chuggin round the bend, feller drivin it along, an that ole feller up on the porch, he rises up, his eyeballs just abuggin an he says,

"maw, git the shawtgun—ah doan know whut hit is, but doan let hit git away"

maw gits don the shawtgun and comes ott, she takes keerful aim and fars

them shawtgun pellets splays all over thatair moll t and that feller adrivin he jumps and jes lights ott across the pasture, the moll t keeps rot on amoseyin don the road

"did ya git hit, maw?"—the ole feller can't see too good

"no paw" she says, lowerin the gun—the moll t amoseyin on don the road—"but ah made it let loos-a that man"

DIARIO Y CARTAS

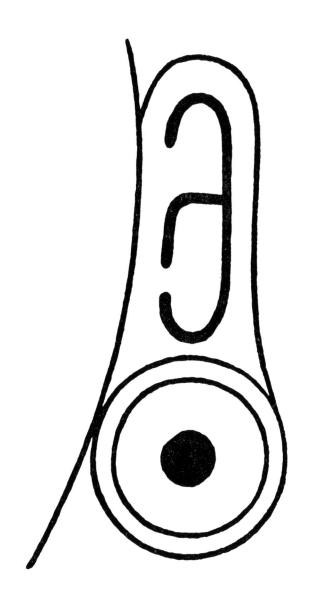

Aloha Bar
Miami International Airport
5 pm   5/18/59
(budweiser)

wall, so mebbe ya got my wire by now, made the western onion man garntee delivery at 6 pm (the witching hour)—

things not too hectic, wms. in a temperate frame, eastern flight very smooth

well, have ya stopped bawlin? I don't understand wimmin—ya beat 'em, cuss 'em, maltreat 'em and when ya leave, they bawl—

coupla hours from now I climb me into a tin can and go like the very wind—

next communique from parts further south

love & stuff

Paul

aw, quit bawlin, I'm comin back

Lunes 18 de Mayo

como una niebla gruesa
el hispanoamericano
cuelga
entre nos y el indio

the carribean is the oak bluffs of south america, a sink trap

flying over the caribean at night, over a flaky layer of clouds—muy hermoso

[93]

heat lightning over Colombia, like it spread the length, the unobstructed alleys of the cordillera, panama to patagonia

funny difference: the U. S. is breadth, S. A. *length*

2:30 AM—
over the pacific

runnin 2 hours late which suits me fine, I'll get to see more o' them handy andes, got a good window seat, east side

panama hot slimy full of furriners slingin' us hammerican tourists the slick eye, glad to be away & above it all—my panamanian plane pal was real palsy, though, I could dig his spanish better than his english, so help me

with the aid of god, seconal & bellows club, I've had one thick hour of sleep, figure that's enough

P.

guayaquil another dirty little place feller took my letter with a dirty look & a rattle of spanish wouldn't even let me buy a stamp & don't believe I sealed it, you got, no?

she-Injun in felt hat and poncho tried to sell me a shawl but I figure I wait

well, I've seen it all a few moments ago: dawn over the andes: might's well turn around at lima & come home

extra stop at Talara, first footing in Peru: a freshness, even though a desert: cool wind, brown sand sterile, but maritime, a pleasure after the thick sticky sick spanish heat of Panama & Guayaquil

and now breakfast, huevos revueltos, revoltin' eggs, that is, and coffee with Pream, the invention of some diabolo norteamericano

———————————

[94]

I have just enjoyed my first southern hemisphere defecation, albeit airborne. I am at home.

Love,

el caballero

Martes 19 de Mayo

Flying just offshore, from Talara to Lima: the garua, the cloudfog obscures ocean & shore completely, the guano islands and the first hills of the mainland emerging from the puffy snowcotton blanket—beyond, to the east, the cordillera negra and the cordillera blanca, glistening

landing at Lima, dipping, as though blindly, into this puffy stuff, real eerie feeling—on the land, all gray, foggy, grunting to rain, and dismal

weird barren brown treeless grassless mountain coastline, and inland, south of Lima—here and there a narrow streambed that hasn't dried up, with strips of farm pursuing it to the sea, pinching it all the way

Lake Titicaca: on a clear sunny winter day the most magnificent body of water, the bluest bluest deepest bluest lapis lazuli indigo cerulean bluest *azul*, makes the rich blue sky pale, it is just unimaginable, the lake & sky, the brown mountains, here is the whole story of the basic colors of so much of Indian design, the brown & blue—if the race didn't originate on these shores, it shoulda knowed better

(on copacabana, there was, antiguamente, an idol of carved lapis lazuli, highly polished)

La Paz a fantastic city, at first it seems sorta brown and unattractive, scattered in its little saucer, but you get into it, walk the streets, nose the shops, etc., and it is fascinating, everywhere the subterranean Indian—cold shadows, warm sun, all buildings wide open, no heat—the american consul complains of the altitude, it makes him dream too much—mixed effect

[95]

of climate and steep streets: to exhilarate & slow, at the same time—mad location & distribution of city, sunk in the midst of the barren hills & upland, you turn down a street and all of a sudden there's that damn brown barrenness again, or maybe a vast snowy peak, as though you could reach & touch

Col. Medina: very possibly the greatest single archeological collection in the world, packed into one room—the immense amount of fine, detailed, minute work—in sculpture & pottery, the facial types of all races; hence, the prime race—Sun god as leader with worshipers, of which there may have been, at least in plan, many more—presence of swastika in tihuanacu design

many wari-wilka (cameloid) types—also, most fabulous along these lines, the twin dinosaurs, goddammit, joined together (see dragon as folk memory of dinosaur)—many phalli, stylized & representational

superb mochica love vase, man & woman caught at it

gold work as fine as the colombian

2 types of trepanning: cutting & rasping—the complete set of surgical tools, of minute gradation, for trepanning—also, the female mummy showing a caesarean

Medina: que hombre—"Una coleccion magnifica, indescriptable, hecho por un caballero verdadero del viejo mundo"—this I write in his guestbook, as we drink a liqueur

20 de mayo
hotel sucre palace
7 ayem

if I tried to give you details of all the superb & unimaginable impressions I received yesterday, I couldn't—so I won't.

[96]

suffice it to say that Lake Titicaca, from the plane, on a brilliant winter day, is just beyond belief—this is THE place in THE world

had excellent conversation with plane pal, Lima to La Paz, a suave frenchman now living in Lima, he gave me much lowdown so that I landed sort of with my feet on the ground

here at sucre palace (the local gentry, I find out, call it sucker's palace) instead of austria, sort of worked out that way

now, La Paz: it is just another one of those things I can't begin to explain, but you might as well start packing—this is, beyond all doubt, THE CITY—incredible

now, Col. Medina, whom I visited yesterday: one of the strangest, most intense, remarkable men, almost dead from sheer physical and mental deterioration and exhaustion, poor as dirt, but with the fire of his posession, his madness—Tihuanacu—burning in him, holding him together —he had a bad cold, he showed me around for a while, went back to his chair, coughed, wheezed, drowsed, opened an eye, saw me looking at something new, he just HAD to come charging out of the chair, a little weary bull, to explain . . . if you can imagine a c---- with a glowing coal, the last spark of the conquistadors driving him, forcing him—que hombre!

his collection is dynamite, incredible—am going back again before I leave—

everything thus far is incredible—which is why I believe it

> throw out your bum ear and
> start packing

> Señor Boliviano

Miercoles 20 de Mayo

T-day: made my arrangements with the taxi man, and we're off—the climb out of the city, etc., and across la puna—harvest time, the injuns digging out the spuds, spreading them to freeze, then turning in the hogs to root what they missed—much barley—as before, this insane geography, them early joes didn't *choose* the blue-brown color scheme, they were *driven* to it—here every fragment of the landscape constantly impels, you're like under a pressure, but distant, again that funny combination of exhilaration and relaxation—about the barley, the injuns use the grain for themselves, feed the rest to the stock, see Carl Sauer (also mebbe Anderson), field & garden one, important to get this in—on to tihuanacu, the ruins themselves at first glance not impressive, but just wait, buster—am impressed again, as at Medina's, with the delicacy of the work, the pieces are not as large, as grandiose as expected—it is this: the intense refinement of a style, over a period of centuries, *clustered* at one place—incredible, the delicacy of the work in this astounding geography—thank god & pachamama for their only begotten son: Sarjento Chura, indio casi puro, devoted student of Posnansky & Medina, another little man, like the colonel, with a hot coal burning in him, he is a guide in more ways than he knows (love his term for the bolivian archeologists: muchachos)—the straightness of those goddamned lines, these were a people who knew something and were organizing it—it is no virtue, size: what began at tihuanacu exploded at the river rouge, the temple kalassaya, be it ½ a futbol field, gives the feeling of delicacy, especially conceived as an instrument (calendarial) (but for that matter you could lose the rouge plant in la puna—and let's do it)—later, a lovely time, drinking beer and smoking my norteamericano cigars with Sarjento Chura and the taxi guy (in his own way, a good joe, asks many pathetic questions about the states) (he bought his chevrolet via New Orleans, they told him it would do very well in La Paz, it was used to the mountains of Louisiana)—the beautiful church of tihuanacu, almost enough to drive a man to god, a huge thing, long, with galvanized tin roof, wooden cross beams, adobe walls, and sculpture and building blocks pilfered from las ruinas—inside, the blue dome (that damn sky again!), the dull old spanish colonial paintings, the gaudy remnants of the fiesta pasada—outside, again, in the sun, in the broad abandoned plaza, (the village dead with poverty), chatting with the padre, the taxi driver, Sarjento Chura (truly we are a gentle troup), the padre pointing out to me the wild, early tiahuanaco sculptured heads, built, for no particular reason, into the high eaves of the church

near the entrance, the figures of the virgin and the piles of rock, catholic and indian, side by side

back to La Paz and Sr. A--- P---, manufacturer, young rich and aggressive, wants nothing more than to live in the states, where he has traveled extensively, t'hell with 'im

the great thing about tiahuanaco and its stone art, it is expuesto to the weather (like the coastal fisherman, to the water)—hence, unlike protected art, it survives

4:30 PM—sucre palace

well when you go out to tihuanaco—the origin of early man in america—what do you expect to find?—two california coeds, doin' the ruins—they talked a slick spanish and took pitchers and gave me a lot of tips about cuzco, how to avoid the tourist traps, etc.—so, the contemporary, together with the most ainshunt

it was quite a day—incredible, the survival of that delicately carved stonework, thru the centuries—location magnificent, sense of the original presence of the lake, the geologic changes, etc.—extra kick, though, was the man: Sarjento Chura, almost pure Indian, local guide, uneducated, poor as dirt, but knows the place in and out, has dug for Posnansky, Medina, Bennett, etc., calls the present Bolivian archeologists "children"—remarkable little man—why do I keep running into people who remind me of c---- but with that extra inner hot coal glowing—convinced it has something to do with tihuanacu itself

so much to say, so little time, etc,—are you packed yet?

[99]

leaving here day after tomorra, you'll be glad to know, boat trip on the lake and RR to Cuzco, if I think of it I might send a cable

---

half hour interruption, went down to the lobby to meet Sr. p----, he's a nuisance, american-type business man, scared to death of r----, I think, I now have to have 2 lunches with him and a tour of the city

---

a moment to remember: chatting outside the church at Tiahuanaco (dig up Posnansky in the studio, there's a beautiful photo of it) with the un-shaven almost poor-as-an-Indian padre, a lovely man, who came out to open the church for me, also Sarjento Chura, and the driver who brought me out (who now seems, after p----, a real good joe)—chatting, in the open spanish-style plaza, almost abandoned, under the goddamdest bluey blue sky

later, drinking beer with Chura, he pours a little on the ground first, for pachamama

ah, there is so much!

el indio puro

my first anti-norteamericano demonstration: a waiter passes behind my back and says to his friend "yanqui!" and they both go giggling into the kitchen

favor de aguadar la llegada which means please keep all these goddam let-ters, I'm putting some things in here which don't get into my notes and visee versee

don't forget your woolies, it gets chile at night

[100]

May 21, 11.30 AM

I'm moving kinda slow today, but I'm moving, it's a joke how it happened: that lousy american vice-consul told me to try the hotel copacabana for food, so I go try it, the food is good, and I order a little white wine to go with, turns out I've bought a whole goddam bottle, by now everyone's staring at me, the waiters giggling, hell, I ain't gonna give in, nothing to do but drink it and walk out like a gentleman which absolutely I do (with chilean wine, the best made anywhere, this is possible) a southern gentleman no less, I pay with a $20 bill U.S. which creates an international crisis and I've got more goddam bolivianos in change, etc., etc.

at six this morning I thought I was dead, but I started blowing on my own little hot coal, and now I'm glowing

all of which proves: we pay the least for things that matter most to us— the most for trash

just found out that I haven't been putting a complete address on my letters to you, they may all be wandering around brazil, some joke, huh?

Jueves 21 de Mayo

Wonderful personal tour of Tiahuanaco Museum by painter-guy—sense of evolution of style, through the periods, in ceramic arrangements— collection not as rich, though, as Medina's—best piece: carved quena, made from condor bone—posnansky's room, fireplace, etc., fine old half-delapidated building—machine-gun chitchat with two painters on the place tihuanacu might occupy in a modern artist's development—feel sorry for them, afraid they don't have an angle on it, they are impelled by it—the straight guys (medina, chura) are cooking on a better (older) fire

p----s not bad, had midday dinner at their home, martinis, wine, beer, etc., p---- and wife and brother, little boy with Roy Rogers pistol little girl with hula hoop—sort of funny to see the split-level ranch-type set grafted onto old Spanish colonialism (Luther Burbank should live so)

[101]

sinister cholo slums, bullet holes of last revolution (month ago), Indian markets, wideopen thieves market, etc.—bargaining for goods

Bolivian landscape, outside city, like Arizona or Utah

Openair park—tihuanacu pieces—sort of dismal, it and I keeping the wrong company—imagine, for god's sake, the great monolito Wendell Bennett in situ, against that Tihuanacoid sky

Moisés Chire Barrientos (*Artist Pintor*) telefono 2239.
Mueso Nacional tihuanacu—La Paz—Bolivia.—

just bought a couple of this guy's paintings, not too bad, he and I are cooking on the same gas, we've both got tiahuanaco in our guts—he has great respect for the work of the present bolivian archeologists

remarks about a pre-tihuanaco civilization, very undeveloped, recently excavated, underneath everything else

Sr. p---'s remark, about the ancient tree trunk, 4 ft. thick, recently excavated, further justification for the lush vegetation theory, antiguamente

send Will Wests to Medina, P----, Barrientos—also, It Is to Barrientos

now, why in hell are the present tihuanacu excavations being sponsored by some *japanese* group?

may 22—ayem

leaving today, just sent you a cable, did ya get it, huh? look forward to mail in kuzzgo

el boliviano

May 22

pleasant shopping tour in the Indian market this morning, stopped in at big dilapidated old San Francisco cathedral, date on it says 1549, guess I'll go see mother quinn about a conversion

[102]

shoeshine in front of cathedral, beggars, Indians, organ music, jeeps, trucks, colectivos—Indians don't believe in autos, walk in middle of the street, must be constantly tooted out of the way, La Paz a city peppered with toots—from a radio in the remote corners of an Indian grotto, Elvis Pressley—

lunch today with p---- then board the train for Guaqui night boat to Puno, train tomorrow for Cuzco—unless I jump ship somewhere, to stay with that goddam lake—

on board ferrocarril La Paz Guaqui: RR travel in bolivia is like minsky's: interminable intermissions while characters come on board and try to sell you trash—

Sabado 23 de Mayo

Sitting in RR car just off the boat at Puno, gray, snow falling heavily, like that insane bolivian blue was centuries away—boy who carried my bags, barefoot, freezing to death, sits and stares at me, wonders what it is to sit and write notes

well, this is a strange world—drinks dinner more drinks last night with 2 serious-bohemian french university students bumming around south america, plus young american slob, ICA, one of those government men down here teaching the bolivians how to be good yankees (muchos weeskee con soda on his expense account)—plus his associate, henrique, bolivian gentleman, real nice, keeping in spite of all hell his dignity (even when he insists we call him hank), all this on top of the world, Lake Titicaca—the only place in the world where you can be seasick and mountainsick at the same time—fine little steamer, we talk international politics, titahuanaco, etc., the world is a strange place

watching the loading of freight, in the titicaca dusk—some kind of mineral in bags—the indians chattering, flying in and out of the hold, their ponchos flapping like batwings—the ICA man commenting, over my shoulder, on their inefficiency

[103]

under way, Peru gray and grimy after bolivia, the Indian poverty without relief, sinister, Pukara a filthy little hole (can't help thinking that the puna-bolivia-titicaca area did something to those around it (tihuanacu) that it still does, despite all hell—but all hell makes upland Peru grimy)

ferrocarril friends: Carmen (muy guapa, muy viva, we have fun) and her sisters (3 peruvian gals on a vacation), and good ole Frank and his gang (Clearwater, Fla.), he has good Spanish, roughed it in Peru 25 years ago as a mining engineer, has come back now with wife and friends to *relive it all*, they sit in perfect isolation, squirt insecticide from time to time, he calls the trip a "course in home appreciation"—we have one end of the car while the La Paz (professional) futbol team—*The Strongest*—has the other

Carmen and her sisters buy me delicious little potato cakes, give me apples, etc.

nice scene with another lovely impoverished padre, on his way to some un-padred little town para hacer un matrimonio, again exchange of cakes and fruits, very festive

snow again at 14,000′ pass, but cleared up—getting better now, vilcañota valley, descending toward Cuzco, the farming makes the land interesting, the barley fields as though wave-washed all the way up the mountainsides, and the river itself, well, enough water will make anything clean, no?

arrival in cuzco in pitch dark, seems the municipal power system is overloaded, every time a thundercloud appears they pull the main switch—the station a madhouse, muchos muchachos trying to grab my bags, I tag after my three gals and we share a taxi—I pay bill, they put on wild scene, involving Cuzco police con flashlight, seems I was being overcharged 10¢, very funny

Hotel Cuzco elegant, spacious, clearly the peruvians are more efficient than the bolivians—the incredible vulgarity of the murals in the dining room—damn good steak

[104]

Domingo 24 de Mayo

Waked up by the bells of Cuzco, and they ain't pretty, more like the puerto rican beer-can serenade in new york—after this, a brass band

Carmen Blossiers, Cortes 166 No. 204 (Department or Floor), Lima, Perú—Will West

Much of Cuzco is gentle, attractive, delightful—unlike brutal, unsettled La Paz—which, I guess, is why I prefer La Paz—amazing how the character of what the spaniards found, at each place, dictated what they created there—which persists today—as, Tiahuanaco→La Paz and Cuzco→ Cuzco (in each case, through 3 periods: Indian, Colonial & now)

Why I don't take photographs: those rocks must be aching from throwing themselves at all that goddam film

Out to Pisac, the market, ruinas, etc., this morning—Pisac sordid, dirty, the market a travesty, with that unenlightened grime I come to associate with Peru—the farm valleys, though, are magnificent, jesus, these incas, in handling agriculture & water (the two being the same) are magnificent

the baño del inca is lovely, you get a sort of shrine feeling in the stonework—ceremonial approach to water *first*: then, its distribution for irrigation, agriculture, use—note the hard rock over which water emerges, showing no erosion (perhaps hardening with the years, like the puerta del sol

Sacsahuaman: very norteamericano, like, how big a rock can we carve and move? a kind of brute sluggishness at the heart of this—

a thought: the "bigness" we put in our works is not so much the size of the land around us—this serves mainly to confirm—as it is the distance from roots, from sources—the dimension of john henry, paul bunyan, the rouge plant, etc., is not that of the space and resource they conquered, but of the atlantic ocean: the distance the mythmakers traveled, to reach

[105]

. . . again and again, at tihuanaco, in the andean vastness, I was impressed that these sculptures are not gross but concentrated, complex, delicate—resourceful . . . look, however, at the massiveness of sacsahuaman and easter island

Just back from the futbol, que partido! "The Strongest" (La Paz) 2, "Lucre" (Cuzco) O, and I'm glad—a beautiful game at this level of skill, the speed, flow, delicacy of manipulation, teamwork make it almost like ice hockey—note the reverse kick, both feet up, and you land on your can—

south america is the last outpost of insanity, it's our only chance

May 24

my latest international bum is a Danish architect out of Toronto, bumming central & south america, we're going to Machu Picchu together Tuesday, he thinks me funny for traveling like a gentleman, staying in hotels, etc., apparently south america is full of jack kerouacs, their only pride is their poverty, their ability to get things for 1/20th what it costs the tourists (me), but it's all so aimless, a desperate sort of exhaustion underlying it

5:30 pm—just back from the stadium (where else?) where I watched the futbol (what else?) very exciting, a good tonic for ruins

Lunes 25 de Mayo

Archeological museum closed for repairs, goddamit, even Clearwater Florida with his bribes and letters of introduction can't get us in—

Mercado Central: greens & bloodmeat & hot smells, all wrapped in dirt, I must be a goddam gennulman, I don't love this dirt for its own sake

Hectic pace of life in these SA cities, it ain't much pretty

South Americans are animals, live, think, eat, compete like animals—

[106]

death is implicit in one misstep, security no existe—culture the product of leisure?—but there is no leisure, so the indian gets dirtier and the spain-blooded struggles to stay afloat, maybe rise enough to get to the states—the cholo sits in the middle and churns (revolts)

there is only one straight line in all south america, one gesture of clarity and distinction: tihuanacu

bolivian beer is good, peruvian beer tastes like rhinegold—but Inca cigarillos are all right

completely norteamericano evening with bunch of young slobs from miami and san diego, feel like now I've got my second (Indian) wind, god dam, let's get out of cuzzgo—

(the horrible bizzness of the shunting aside of the wellmeaning peruvian gentlemen, the one who worked to get the coca for the detroit bitch, and the other who went out of his way to get the information on the larco herrera museum for me, their hearth, hotel, etc., pre-empted) (at least more theirs than ours)

it's a question of energy: at anywhere near the exhaustion level, south america is impossible—there must be enthusiasm—south america being the chaos of ourselves, this is important

May 25

3 of us together in hotel at Machu Picchu, Pete the Dane, Don the New Yorker (met him on train out this morning), and me—I must say it's pretty god damn impressive, nothing I've seen in pictures has given me a sense of it, the purity of color (this is where those photographers, damn 'em, tell lies, LIES!) and those goddam stalagmite mountains all around —they have done a remarkable job of leaving it pure and clean

Martes 26 de Mayo

PETER STUDSGARTH, SØBORGHUSPARK 9, SOBORG, DEN-MARK—compañero de machu picchu

[107]

Lima: El Patio Restaurant (near Plaza de Armas)
    Norte Pacifico Bus (near Bolivar Hotel)
    Granada restaurant
    Chiappi—avenida pierola (cheap, italian, good)
    El Vencedor—125 Jiron Cuzco
(above information provided, in advance, by Don Leinbach)

Miercoles 27 de Mayo

Machu Picchu—from huayna picchu, the peak, how much impressive —the tall **peaks all around, the** guard points up & down river, the needle sharp mountains—the vastness of the thing, spreading over its crown, its saddle, at the crucial point—climbing huayna picchu—Don, Pete & I—straddling the ridge, 2000′ straight down on either side—at the right moment, after sunset, the condor flight—the beautiful greenness of these mountains, almost tropical, but rising to snow peaks—the rockwork: the city emerging from the living rock, many great boulders, uncarved or partially carved—one carved up to the top, where it is left in the shape of mountains—machu picchu spring water now used in the hotel, the best I've had in South America—beautiful train ride with Don Leinbach, Machu Picchu to Cuzco, on the platform all the way (against rules but brakeman didn't bother us)—view of Ollantay-tambo, terraces, etc., massive—delicious tangerines, bananas, oranges (lunch for 2, 6¢)

machu picchu sunrise: the first pink touch on the snow caps—you wouldn't believe it, pal

the high points thus far: tihuanacu & the puna, and machu picchu & the mountains—(also, medina)

back in Cuzco: playing bumper pool with Arturo and Rojer, peruvian caballeros—they let me win—nothing will take the place of manners, suh

Machu Picchu: wild strawberries, and many flowers—the hotel manager's kids playing futbol in the open court

[108]

May 27

Just back in Cuzco—more later

May 27

yes, machu picchu, machu picchu, god dam, you have to see it to believe it—

beautiful ride back to cuzco on the filthy indian train, on the platform all the way—sunshine, magnificent scenery

these travel friendships you make are delightful, and fortunately they come to an end, on to the next

Jueves 28 de Mayo

the indians liked to pick a spectacular spot and then get just behind it—para ocultar—this true, certainly, of machu picchu, probably chavín & san agustín

yesterday, the filthy indian train from Machu Picchu—today, Aviacion Fawcett, DC-4 to Lima—life here, like the mountains, is tilted, faulted and stratified—I slice it like fruit cake—nowhere as in S.A. is individual character impressed against its background, framed, clarified—personality emerges with a sharpness as terrifying as the geography

On plane, Cuzco to Lima: lady across the way, clutching her oxygen tube and her beads, together—getting it both ways

Passing 21,000′ mountains, close by—oh, it's vurry drum attic—

May 28

just arrived hotel maury, very nice, cheaper than advertised—flight down quick, easy, right past 21,000 ft. snow peaks—going Machu Picchu-to-

[109]

Cuzco-to-Lima is strange, the reverse of Miami-to-Tiahuanaco, like I was shot out of a cannon (Zacchini) into the present, Lima big, modern, commercial, it's just impossible to imagine the contrasts in this continent, nothing comparable—all South America shut down today for Corpus Christi, I may not be able to mail this until tomorrow

May 28—11 PM

well, this time it's a funny little student from San Marcos University, picked me up on the street when I was looking for the airline office, learning english (they all are), loves norteamericanos (they all do), took me to the movies (Frank Sinatra, Dean Martin, what else?), drinks, dinner, drinks, I had to fight to pay the dinner check, etc., is gonna take me to the museum, pachacamac, everything, all weekend, I feel somehow I'm taking advantage, to him I'm the biggest thing that's hit since Nixon

Lima is Lima. if they spoke a little more english, it would be Miami.

have just found out I go monday by camioneta (pickup truck, oh boy) to Huarás, will cable

what's the popular soft drink here? of course: Inka Kola

your letters, plus anniversary card, all waiting for me here, muy buenas, maybe, who knows, someday you'll get some of mine—

picked up 2 chiggers in machu picchu, no place like home

May 29

Roger—my buddy—laid up this morning with "dolor de cabeza" (hangover), so I do errands, get information, etc.—on way back to hotel, get involved in street demonstration, revolutionary sympathizers, shopkeepers hustling to slam doors, pull iron bars over windows, demonstrators in tight formation, cavalry charges, throws tear gas, they—and I—disperse, *muy rapido*, just a quiet latin american morning—

[110]

out to Pachacamac, 20 miles south, hill & ruins on the coast, magnificent location, whole pacific ocean at your feet—the weather never clears in Lima in the winter, but today it was sunny and bright, nobody understood but me—

Roger expert & generous guide, but he begins to be a nuisance, he gets tanked every night & maudlin, I must be the whole magnificent U. S. A. to him—he of course had never seen Pachacamac, didn't know it was there, tried hard to understand why I cared—tragic spanish eyes, brooding, in a kid so happy he can say "ruck 'n' rull"—a spanish gentleman, about to be fractured

well, on soon elsewhere

happy anniversary!

Viernes 29 de Mayo

as far as Limeñans are concerned, the Rio Rimac runs the wrong way, from the mountains they take nothing, turn their backsides to them, and their faces to the movie screen

but in Lima, you can smoke an Inca, light it with a Llama, while you drink an Inca Kola—

nice feeling in hotel maury—even though remodeled—of being one of many extranjeros viajando en el perú—they have the fine old espejos de luna, comedor and lobby—

street demonstration, revolutionary sympathizers, cavalry, tear gas, etc. —what the hell am I doing here, anyway?

institute of contemporary art, exhibition of one Ricardo Grau, slick coastal modernism, a faint touch of the indian in his colors, but it all looks like fingernail polish

[111]

best south american meal yet, Granada Restaurant, Don Leinbach's recommendation, sopa criolla, liza con ensalada, cerveza aleman—

Lima is a cleaner city, fewer beggers, but one feels the grind, the animal scarce veneered—

Pachacamac: again, as always, it is location: indentation in the coast, with the desert correspondingly in the mountains, imposing hill, guano island offshore, magnificent command, almost "possession" of that dark goddam ocean—extension, spread of the city, much of Frank Lloyd Wright in the terraces, walls, etc.—as with Machu Picchu, it is the distant view that makes it

here, even in bright sunshine, the colors are pastel: mountains, desert, ocean, sky

birds: gallinazo, ugly buzzard-type, and lechuza, nocturnal, que trae mal suerte

words, described in the shrubbery: "soy puta." Roger carefully destroys, saying "I'm doing this for the peruvians, not the norteamericanos, everyone knows the norteamericanos can't read spanish."

Roger, orphan boy, adds his scribbling to the others on the adobe bricks: "Mi abuelo vivió aquí." He didn't, really.

Road south out of Lima is *exactly* like Detroit-to-Dearborn: an unsettled people squatting on a desert

a thought: early man was a hunter, living in nomadic hordes, following game—the great event of culture, of civilization, was a process of *rooting*, of acquiring *place*: a fishing group (Humboldt Current?), stationary on land by virtue of the fishrich ocean, spreading, experimenting into agriculture (*rooting*)—this led to astronomy, study of the seasons, in the modern sense, *knowledge*—hence, an aristocracy (knowledgeable group) and *centres of knowledge*: Tihuanacu, Chavín, San Agustín,

Pachacamac—*to know, one must root*—now, thanks to the Incas (Roman) (spread of knowledge) (welfare state) (colonizing, uprooting local cultures)—and Ford—we are once more nomadic—

Pachacamac: it is that magnificent sense of the *right* location: this is not a gesture, but a matter thought with precision

me, a yankee, eating a chinese dinner in lima, peru, while the band plays the blue danube—what I mean, native culture

all south americans can say "sawnawvabeech" and "boolsheet," and some of them can say "cawksookare"

May 30—9 PM

well, Roger had to turn out to be what he is, which god made him, and I ain't—which all, I suppose, goes with Lima—again, the spanish gentleman came to his aid, there was a scene, but a clean scene—by the way, did you ever turn down a fairy in spanish?

incidentally, you don't have to worry about the gold standard, I seem to have no economy at all—who knows, this is the end of everything, maybe?

tomorrow at 3/30 am they call me (this is the strangest goddam continent) and at 4 I go by "colectivo" (taxi that you share with 4 other people and costs practically nothing) all the way to Huarás—later in the week, Chimbote, Trujillo, etc.—looks like I'll make the goddam trip in about 4 weeks, frightening, isn't it?

Sabado 30 de Mayo

To the museum today, magnificent collection, fine spanish patio type building (but I miss that tumble down old building in La Paz)—best stuff the chavín, as in tiahuanaco, strength & delicacy, combined: feline conflations—snakes with fangs, felines condorclawed—

[113]

phalloliths, elliptic, glyphed

estela raimondi a great piece: the indian continuous, the generations joined, mouth to crown, mask to mask, in the headdress—the phallic tongue a river, passing name and race

superb textiles, paracas, over & over repetition of blue-brown motifs, sense of red purified out of red-brown earth—collections of other colors more common in U.S., they are not typical, representing rather the collector's taste

monolitos from Casma, suggesting both tiahuanaco & chavín—

Roger M---- — Will West — and so much for that

Domingo 31 de Mayo

Wild colectivo ride, Lima to Huarás, ugly cholo driver, violent indian-spanish-peruvian scenery, interminable goddam moonscape, desert, rocks, straw & adobe huts, dry as dust, nothing, nothing, nothing—delicious 28¢ beefsteak breakfast—filthy, almost haunted little town where we stopped for the control, radio blaring ruck 'n' rull—climbing then, gradual return of green, as we get to where the rains can reach

and now the Hotel Monterrey, a day of rest, swiss & precious in this weird continent: clean room, good food, swimming pool, mineral baths, genteel american missionaries to talk to, etc., all unreal

every place I visit produces an indigenous personality type by way of companion, even those who travel seem to present themselves to me in the place that naturally, incisively frames them—it is this, the place-sense, the background at all times pushing, projecting, that gives to human personality here an at times well nigh insane clarity, precision

Monday, June 1

this little hotel is incredible—am sitting now on the terrace overlooking

[114]

a border of flowers, swimming pool, weeping willow, eucalyptus, mountains, etc., air fresh & clear, sun warm, cute little peruvian chick sitting
next to me—later today, a trip to Huarás for the museum, and maybe a
swim—tomorrow, Chavín, in the hotel station wagon (chick's poppa in
offing, don't worry)

tea yesterday with 4 american missionaries, they know somebody named
Innes who has a chicken farm on Starne's Cove Road, Asheville, N. C.—
one of them lost a brother to the headhunters a while back, I'm in favor
of this sort of thing

another author-type here, swiss, he sits out on the terrace with his type-
writer—competition

———————————

just back from a walk down the road—fun saying "buenas tardes" to all
the indians, watching the reaction—they had to go empty and clean the
swimming pool today, so no swim—instead, I went down and sat by the
river—

Lunes 1 de Junio

Huarás beautiful, the loveliest I've seen in South America—everything
that Cuzco claims to be and isn't—as Cuzco fronts for Machu Picchu,
so Huaráz for Chavín—a nonnection here?

the autos here in the little streets (calles estrechísimas) are quaint, not
ruthless—there is a survival of spanish leisureliness

beautiful faces, the most beautiful women in south america, these people
haven't been slashed by the harshness—even a puta, glorious

not antinorteamericano, the first time I haven't felt a hardness—curious,
polite

poverty here, but gentle, no starvation, the land too rich—in La Paz &
Cuzco, one feels the grindstone daily casts out hulls—

[115]

lovely waiter, Hotel Monterrey, heard me last night talking, in english, about tiahuanaco & chavín, wants to make sure I get to the museo here in Huarás—I reached *him*, if not the missionaries

just realized, Roger M---'s whine for "service" was the same whine used by the beggars—

indian funeral, everyone talking, laughing, the casket a light burden— must have been a cholo, they're glad he's dead

the south american fruitcake: the indian at the bottom, doing the work, turning out the food, etc.; then the cholo—he drives taxis and buses, waits on table, tends store, anything uncreative and, if possible, destructive; next, the spanish colonial, who used to be boss but who has now been superseded by the yankee, descending from the north via panagra, radio-active fallout, the real topdog

sign on the front of a camion: si dios quiere, volveré

another: amarte es mi delirio

Martes 2 de Junio

damn, this waiter's making a big thing about my getting to the museum, "ojalá" he says "ojalá"—it's like his ancestry is at stake, everything depends on my getting the right impression—hope I don't disappoint him—

just back from museo, will say what I can, which is mostly the magnificent vistas, the primitive monolitos in rows in the patio, against the flowers, the spanish wall, and in the background the magnificent cordillera blanca, huascarán, etc.—after a while, the little monolitos seem to be people, so many intelligent monkeys, watching

ride to chavín worth the price, even if there were nothing there to see— climbing to snowline, tunnel through the cordillera blanca, descending other side, interminable switchbacks, descent to one of those marvelous, warm, rich valleys east of the andes, giving toward the selva

[116]

chavín at first sight a shambles, thanks to the ministerio de whatever it is, but swinging around to the river, the ball court or whatever, you get an idea, magnificent block of condors, 7 running toward the jefe, almost in the style of tihuanacu, but distinto—this business of influence very touchy, the similarity intense but at the same time the individuality intense: if they did take from the boys to the south—as it appears—they sure god made it their own

you find the guy with the key and start crawling around the underground vaults, fine pieces, original of monolito tello, smaller tiahuanacoid pieces —crawl on your belly through a 2 x 2 hole and come to a room with camarones carved on the ceiling, and there it is: camerones are found only in the rivermouths on the pacific coast: this valley gives east, to the selva, but chavín gave west, to the coast—*over* those two goddam mountain ranges—them dam shrimp, hiding on the ceiling, this is the height of the occult, the mysterious

manager of Hotel Monterrey drove me over, I got to know him pretty well, almost spoiled the whole hotel for me—we killed a dog and a chicken on the way, would have killed indians if they hadn't jumped fast ("indians aren't people, they're animals" he sez)—I can take this stuff from cholos, they have blood reasons, but not from a goddam swiss—of course he hates it here, can't wait to get out to europe or the states

Miercoles 3 de Junio

The western hemisphere is a man: patagonia—pie grande—the foot: tihuanacu—between the legs, the two cordilleras—the generative: mas al norte—brazil, etc.—the cuerpo: and u. s. a., the head, the sense of it all . . . it is with this geographic man that, as hombre americano, I am possessed

> a man dropped,
> airwelled
> to the patagoni

> (bigfoot at the bottom)

[117]

to rise through gran chaco
amazonas
coclé

to spread:
        toltec, texan
                pueblo north american

scarey roads, hard driving, magnificent scenery, Huarás to Chimbote—crossing the cordillera negra, at the very top, an indian boy pissing, no hiding, a celebration, for us—boy, piss, bus, all the world, the top of the world—

the feeling, the touch of the condor stone, chavín—

        when you incise the rock
        cut it sharp
        cut it deep
                then turn loose
                the alluvium

sanitary rule, south america: always wash your hands before picking your nose

nice young chino-peruano on the colectivo, he carries huge picture of Clark Gable, we talk across the sleeping drunks, he assures me that my spanish pronunciation is lousy, I'm assured

there is much fine modern stonework on peruvian roads, adaptation of ancient methods, use of living rock, etc.—one beautiful example, fullness and refinement, on road Huaráz to Casma

Hotel Trujillo
8:30 PM—June 3

just arrived, your 5 letters and cable waiting for me, feel like I'm on my way home

[118]

tell anne I've met some wonderful priests here, if she wants to marry one it's okay with me, and tell adrienne I've been drinking beer here with honey's father

today, another day of scarey roads, hard driving, magnificent scenery

colectivo ride, chimbote to trujillo, with drunk indian asleep on my shoulder—very restful

about colombian bandits, will go to bogotá, inquire at u.s. consulate, also lalley's friends, be guided accordingly—everything else has been so great, would shoot myself if I missed san agustín—don't worry, this cookie can take care of himself

Jueves 4 de Junio

Trujillo—a slimy charleston-type coastal city—eye doughnut lock day cussed a pea rue—

big excitement of the day: cops on bicycle chasing a thief—they cotch

herrera musem, like everything else in peru, gone to lima—local museum I cannot find, don't care enough to ask, the hell with it, I drink beer instead

chino-peruano friend again, claims to be peruvian fbi-man, trailing smugglers, etc., who knows, maybe so

funny shoulder-rubbing in government hotels, norteamericanos, they come to work, they come to play—slacks, sport shirts, zipper jackets, etc.—and local peruvian uppercrust, rotary club or whatnot, dressed to the hilt, shirts crackling with starch—the yankee sprawls, the peruvian gentleman, unable to be himself in his own hotel, retreats finally into icy reserve

lima-trujillo-charleston-oak bluffs: all ports of llegada and salida are sink traps, serve to deceive as to the nature of what they serve

[119]

only us northers can afford to be candid—formalities are the solace—and revenge—of the underprivileged

I keep going back to the first experience: plummeting out of the modern sky into medina's sanctum of pre-geologic origins: the day that had everything, from dawn over the andes, garua in Lima, that goddam lake, to liqueurs with precious, hot, little coronel federico diez de medina—everything I've done since has in a way been a confirmation of that first day

chan-chan a ghost city, the filthy gallinazos perching & crapping (white craps on the land waves) on the crumbling walls (climbing on which I contribute to the delapidation)—as at chavín, but worse, a sense of delapidated disregard

the taxidriver's two phrases in english: all reet, and les go—serve for all purposes

a weirdness, a ghostliness to this whole coast, the rain that overhangs and never materializes

chan-chan: the original vastness, houses and open courts, can only imagine what a garden steady water would make this—the city spreading almost to the seaside, the faintly damp seabreeze, roar of the surf

the little fragments that bring it back, the signo escalanodo, the bird figure, what it must have been: the imposition of a unified idea of order on a ruthless geography

Trujillo—June 5

THE GIRL WHO TALKED WITH GOD

sitting in the plaza last evening, listening to the band concert, watching the teenagers walking around, one of whom, a she, gets up nerve to come up and ask me, you're not from here, are you? and I say, no, and she says, from where? and I say, the united states, and she says, a-h-h-h-h-h, flutters, well nigh faints, can say no more

[120]

Chiclayo—3 PM

the goddam tourist hotel that shows on the esso map isn't built yet, so I'm staying at a funny little place called hotel europa, real good food —discovered a delicious dark beer called maltina, they say it's very nootrishus

chiclayo I like—maybe it's just that the sun shines, but there's a nice shaded plaza, the breezes blow, and the town doesn't have that filthy old-spanish pretentiousness of lima and trujillo

two letters from you before I left trujillo—including dad's—how's the alfalfa, with all that-there rain?

just found out I have to take a bus at 5 ayem tomorrow, oh, boy

no, I ain't goin' down the amazon, it would be an expensive bit of sight-seeing—for no particular purpose—have been convinced by many that my iquitos-leticia connection is too risky in this uncertain world—so, another few days & dollars saved

there's an esso distributor in trujillo named F. A. Harman, yup, that's the way he spells it

Viernes 5 de Junio

hora peruana: the time things actually happen, not when they say they will

funny sounds in S.A.: church bells, revolution or plumbing?

chiclayo: usual crop of highbreasted beauties, swinging their hips through the erected male glances in full flight

in a restaurant: an ancient asthmatic, scarfed, hobbling—each breath followed by a period and a long pause: like a fish flopping, dying, in the bottom of the boat—comes in, and orders, for survival, a coca cola

[121]

oh how these characters love noise, just noise: church bells, unmuffled motors, radios, p.a systems, dice cups (beat 'em on the table for luck) and most of all, oh, most of all, the goddam human tongue

glimpse into a doctor's office: picture on the wall showing the various vital organs—very convincing

glance at a printshop: bearded christ-like character working at a press in a 2 x 4 cuartito, pictures of christ on the wall—chiclayo jargon?

damn I like this chiclayo, mebbe I was just in the mood for it, but this is a hot little town

Sabado 6 de Junio

negro-peruano, heaving me an insult at 5 ayem: italiano!—then he turned around and clipped me for 10 soles, fake excess baggage charge

bus day, Chiclayo-Piura-Talara—excellent breakfast at La Choza, open-air bamboo-style roadside restaurant, genuine tropical feeling

the game's getting bigger: today we killed a cow—look on the driver's face, sad & gritty, as he drove on

spot on this page is sacred: beer spilled at the Bar of the Royal Hotel, Talara, Peru, a seaside tropical joint to be remembered—rambling old hotel—two frame structures joined together—at the edge of the harbor, view of tugboats and little lateen-sail rigs, makes me feel woppish, like, say, Ezra's first trip over

Talara a "modern" town, full of U.S.-type houses for the petroleo workers—who somehow manage to live in them like peruanos—the Royal Hotel on the edge of all this, a real antidiluvian (ante-american) (but not anti-american) JERNT—architects could labor for years and not get with the style of these two ramshackle shacks, rammed together—the right way to leave peru, almost redeems this whole dull coast—

[122]

few words with peruvian west-pointer, seems like, god bless 'im, he was born in texas—

mad scene in Royal Hotel Bar—peruvian army officer, talking much of U.S.-Peruvian friendship, admires my expensive (cuzco) dark glasses, gracefully pockets same—I say nothing, but later complain to first lieutenant, peruvian police, who asks tactfully (drunkenly) for them, is denied drunkenly (tactfully) (glasses bulging in pocket) that they exist—result: another bit of u.s. foreign aid, much beer, no glasses, no love lost —hail & farewell, peru!

police lieutenant admits to me that he doesn't like Talara, it isn't Peru, too many norteamericanos—more and more it becomes apparent that we (U.S.) lie, horizontally, with no vertical penetration, on top of peru—an added complication to the catholic-on-top-of-indian structure

Talara

bus ride today, chiclayo to talara, you see this coast once and you've seen it all

bus buddies: a slick little red-headed peruvian floozie and a sharp little italiano, lives now in venezuela, traveling salesman type—their's obviously an arrangement, but I didn't seem to interfere with their plans, so we lunched together—they spoke clear spanish for me, mumbly spanish among themselves

in haste, must get to panagra and P.O.

mañana, bogotá

caramba!

Domingo 7 de Junio

Walk down to the pacific this morning, first time—water mild—join

[123]

romantic-maritime-looking boys to watch docking of "esso norfolk," tanker—scene eugene o'neilish

Flying again, panagra, avianca, etc.—rubbing shoulders, lunching, drinking, etc., with assorted fools, tourists and business men, from guess where? the u. s.—best part of flight: departure from talara, view of town, ocean, hotel, etc.

arrival bogotá after dark, looks bigger, sharper than lima—hotel granada full of futbol players, no room, so I pick up my mail and follow hack to funny little pension-type hotel crillon—quien sabe, muy bueno, no? anyway, a solid dinner—tomorrow, to find out about buses & bandits, etc.

Lunes 8 de Junio

Bogotá less spanish, snappier than Lima, more New York than Miami, the layers deeper buried—you feel the proximity of the Great White Father, to the north—the occasional beat Indian on the street more a stranger—first city I am not stared at—

really, the only place the u. s. is attractive is in the u. s., abroad we are something awful to behold—

well, the word is that the bandits ain't banditting south of neiva, so mañana put on my old duds hide my watch my wealth and head for san agustín

u. s. embassy bogotá most u.s.-looking goddam place you ever did saw— all plush and chrome, clean as no blowed whistle ever was—but they done treated me right, ah kent complane

Monday AM—Bogotá

good talk with consul, he say little or no risk, so I go—RR or air thru danger zone, no difficulty from Neiva south—maybe you get cable from me?

[124]

it looks now like I home about a week from today, no?

Martes 9 de Junio

Avianca Bogotá to Neiva, bus Neiva to Pitalito, no further than this I can go today, wait until noon tomorrow and San Agustin only 21 miles away

Colombia much different from Peru and Bolivia, settled, green, etc., the geography less drastic—paved roads, barbed wire (in Peru, an eight-year-old girl fences cattle)—travel generally more settled, less scarey, despite tales of bandeleros

country road, corn & banana patches, hogs, burros, brahma bulls, lovely tile- or thatch-roofed adobe houses, split-bamboo fences—all of a sudden-like, a farmhouse made of aluminum

Pitalito: the inevitable beercan church bells

but the central plaza is lovely, well tended, and the church itself a nice building

no electricity tonight, so the girls bring candles—bet they had 'em saved for church

Tuesday PM—Hotel Monaco
Pitalito, Colombia

Well I aims one way or another to be back in Bogotá by Saturday afternoon, on time to get Avianca's $75 excursion flight to Miami, spend the night there, and fly into Asheville Sunday, no? maybe you got my cable this morning

funny scene in this hotel when I landed, they had one room where the bed wasn't made up, other where the water wouldn't work—great crisis until I solved: move bedding into room where water works—so here I am

[125]

Miercoles 10 de Junio

The lovely Hotel Monaco, they knock on my door at 7:15 a.m., bring me orange juice and coffee (room & board & all this, $1.80 a day)

beautiful breakfast, caldo, eggs in individual little pan, bread, plus a big cup of hot chocolate

guy tells me, don't try to hotel in san agustín, rough, so I go out in the rain with muchacho, find taxi, we make deal, sesenta pesos, for this afternoon, bueno, do it all and return pitalito

nice in the morning, lean on the railing on the hotel balcony, watch the town come alive

vegetable market, rainy, muddy, everything fresh & green, bueno

in colombia they know the u.s. must be listening, they've mufflered their motors

magnificent midday dinner—reminded of filthyrich u.s.-er warning me, cali airport, "don't go anywhere in colombia you can't fly"—flying, amigo, is for the birds

en route san agustín: rich rainrich land, like w.n.c. but without the harsh winter—hard to imagine poverty here, must take extremes of collective mismanagement to achieve it

great idea, pursuing a river to its source—nacimiento—as did them indios the magdalena—the land gets exciting, the cut of the river, the knees of land pushing into it, the waterfalls, and above this, a sweeping arable upland: the place to build

San Agustín: primitivo: the force, at its best

the rock, emerged, conceived first as phallus, and from the head of phallus, emerging, sculpturewise, the head of man

[126]

man himself, todo, as phallus—symbol, staff of authority, headdress, the head itself a dress to the body, as to the phallus

the great work is the work of great heads

emphasis on the mouth, things emerging, extension of tongue—raimondi stela, chavín, and posnansky, flight of the voice—

tongue, speech, phallus, as continuity of the race

the tongue, the race, the phallus, the flute—speech, seed, music

semi-tropics, wild-colored birds, a thing flashing red and yellow, etc.

lavapatas (like the baño del inca) the rocks carved, serpents, etc., serpentine canals, the water directed so that it flows over the carved figure, the god, perpetually washed, cleaned

as in the little outdoor museum in huarás, the feeling that the figures, the clusters of figures, are alive, watching: this the power they gain from being outdoors, as was, as is

the absolute isolation, absolute concentration of these central sites, sitios, all of 'em—essential, this sense of *place* for anything above random rambling—pound's "rose in the steel dust," a focus, a locus

magnificent arrangement of park, wonderful sense you get—from things being left where discovered, almost scarce excavated—of being in on it all, like, this is how it was, the dirt, the land, the place, the thing

> is
> of itself,
> and grows,
> in place . . . (in situ

San Ag a demonstration of how it can be done

nice scene with park director, Sr. Guerrero, when I brought out magazine

[127]

article with pictures of himself and family—called all the family (beautiful wife) they gathered around, he ordered muchacho to serve me as guide, show me everything—like I said before, nice places attract nice people: the warm-eyed muchacho, who had to talk to me about his father: mi papá está en Venezuela, he sez—they all are, son

Hotel Monaco: at first I thought this place was run by a bunch of teenage girls, but I finally met the manager, speaks good english, seems he went to high school in a place called detroit, michigan

after the breakthrough on the english gambit, I now have many friends in the joint—after supper, I give english lessons to all the kids—

Jueves 11 de Junio

lluvia lluvia lluvia para regresar—hoy, pitalito a neiva, por bus—

later, it clears up, the sun comes out, the mountains get kinda pretty

big deal this morning with Sr. Edmundo Aljach Zajar, manager of the Hotel Monaco—he speaks english, spanish, french and arabic, has lived colombia, u.s. & beirut, I'm to bail him outa pitalito, get him a job in the u.s., oy vay—but a nice little guy, I'll try, I'll try

now the hotel tayrona, neiva, poco más moderno, no?

big fat china-colombiana, camarera, the way she floats into the room— her eyes out of chichen itza

Viernes 12 de Junio

oy, what a night—the beauties of open spanish hotel architecture, todo expuesto a todo, what the radioactive hispanoamericano does to this

hoy, neiva a bogotá, por avion

at the airport, neiva: business men are the same everywhere

[128]

bogotá: horrible semi-destroyed reproductions of san agustín figures, sinking in the mud between the billboards, highway from the airport to town

tickets, money, cambio, etc., u.s. embassy again to convince the fools that colombia is safe (earn their salaries for them), then a coupla lousy french movies, to kill time

Sra. M----, and her two boys who went to asheville school, well if this ain't home, it's just about

I like the hotel granada, it once was and it ain't and it's trying to still be, I like the lady because she makes no concessions to my ignorance of span-ish, tough

wild night, last of the trip, with compania colombiana petroleo, or some-such, pretty decent guy, native—like everybody else, in a peck of trouble —really the best of the "contemporaries" I've met, appropriate for last night—solid perception, without rancour, of the idiocy of u.s. position in south america

Sabado 13 de Junio

in bed 5 a.m. muchos weeskee con agua, up at 9 fresh as the proverbial, ham'n'egg breakfast, ready to roll

cambios, cambios, cambios, cheques de viajeros, pesos, dólares, etc.— god bless exprinter cook wagons-lits first national city bank of new york, etc.

national museum bogotá a waste of time, nice building inferior collection, really the only thing in colombia is san agustín

tonight, my lovely, I bed me down in miami

mad business of the lost bag in the taxi, desperate trip in 1948 Ford (35 m.p.h. top speed) 12 miles back to bogotá, chasing, no luck, back to

[129]

aeropuerto (35 m.p.h.) rush thru despecho, aduana, etc., bag given up for lost—at last minute, two taxi guys rush in, bag in arms, first guy had gone back to bogotá, found it in back seat, come back out to find me: saludos, abrazos, handshakes, dólares, pesos, etc., avianca anuncia la salida de vuelo seis seis seis a vecinos de miami, abordo, abordo

slick chick on plane, bogota to baranquilla—baranquilla no hay, sez I, vamos a miami

baranquilla to miami, homely indiana type, abe lincoln without a beard

spraying the plane with insecticide just before arrival, u. s. public health service regulation, get us all good & sterile

miami, customs, taxi, motel, etc.—rum & coke with eastern air lines student pilot, he lends oido simpático to my much unloading

I keep thinking of the lovely guy in bogotá, petroleo, looking in his wallet after another big bar bill, *cada vez menos*, he says, the tenderness, the delicacy, the galloping sadness of the man, like the indian woman, a heap of rags and filth, squatting in the patio, cuzco correos, digging with a pin at the cut, the open running sore on the sole of her foot

> bulking in her stealth
> aloof in public
> huddling, huddling
> flocked in
> hush
>
> flesh a filth
> mountainskirts and bowlerhat
> downthrust
> black black eyes

like the lavapatas at san agustín and the baño del inca in cuzco, the water
running out, pouring over the delicate surfaces, deep cut—

Domingo 14 de Junio

lousy coffee, miami restaurant, I know I'm in the states

eastern air lines, miami to atlanta, standby for flight to asheville, abordo
at the last minute—

a volver

POSTLUDE

between the writing and publication of this book, two charac-
teristically south american events have occurred:

el strongest—the futbol team—has been wiped out in a plane
crash

and the superbly beautiful town of huarás has been devastated by
an earthquake

in memorium: huarás

&

el strongest

BIBLIOGRAPHY

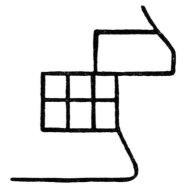

Many of the chapters in this book are obvious conflations of other men's work—I am grateful to the many who went before me, who reported what they saw and did.

Rather than attach burrs to the bottom of each page, I am listing my sources here . . . naturally, many other books were consulted—this list is by no means a recommended bibliography—but for one reason or another (often the disciplines of my own book) their material didn't appear in the finished work, and have not been listed.

SOUTH AMERICA

Acosta, Father Jose de. *Natural and Moral History of the Indians.* London, 1879.

Acuña, Father Christoval de. *A New Discovery of the Great River of the Amazons.* Trans. C. R. Markham, Hakluyt Society, London.

Agassiz, Professor and Mrs. Louis. *A Journey in Brazil.* Boston, 1868.

Alexander, Hartley Burr. *The Mythology of All Races: Latin American.* Boston, 1920.

Arber, Edward (editor). *The first three English books on America.* Birmingham, 1885.

Arguedas, Jose Maria, and Ruth Stephan. *The Singing Mountaineers.* Austin, Texas, 1957.

Ashmead, P. H. *The Madeira-Mamore Railway.* Pan American Union, Washington, 1911.

Bandelier, A. F. "The Aboriginal Ruins at Sillustani, Peru," *American Anthropologist,* Vol. 7, No. 1, 1905.

———. *The Islands of Titicaca and Koati.* New York, 1910.

Barcroft, Binger, Bock, Doggart, Forbes, Harrop, Meakins and Redfield. *Observations upon the effect of high altitude. . . . Philosophical Transactions of the Royal Society of London,* Series B, Vol. 211, London, 1922.

Bates, Henry Walter. *The naturalist on the River Amazons.* London, 1863.

Beals, Carleton. *Fire on the Andes.* Philadelphia & London, 1934.

Bingham, Hiram. *Across South America.* Boston, 1911.

———. "Further Explorations in the Land of the Incas," *National Geographic Magazine,* Washington, 1916.

———. *Inca Land.* Boston & New York, 1922.

———. *Machu Picchu, a Citadel of the Incas.* New Haven, 1930.

————. *Lost City of the Incas*. New York, 1948.

Bird, J., and L. Bellinger. *Paracas Fabrics and Nazca Needlework*. National Textile Museum, Washington, 1954.

Bollaert, W. *Antiquarian, Ethnological and Other Researches in New Granada, Ecuador, Peru and Chile*. London, 1860.

Bouger, M. *An Abridged Relation of a Voyage to Peru*, in *Pinkerton's Voyages and Travels*, Vol. 14. London, 1813.

Bowman, Isaiah. *The Andes of Southern Peru*. New York, 1916.

Brown, John. *Two Against the Amazon*. New York, 1953.

Brown, Rose and Bob. *Amazing Amazon*. New York, 1942.

Bushnell, G. H. S. *Peru*. New York, 1957.

Catlin, George. *Rambles Among the Indians of the Rocky Mountains and the Andes*. London, 187–?.

Church, George E. *Aborigines of South America*. London, 1912.

Cieza de Leon, Pedro de. *The First Part of the Chronicle of Peru*. Hakluyt Society, London, 1864.

Cole, George R. Fitz-Roy. *The Peruvians at Home*. London, 1884.

Cook, O. F. "Staircase Farms of the Ancients," *National Geographic Magazine*, Washington, 1916.

Craig, Neville. *Recollections of an Ill-Fated Expedition*. Philadelphia, 1907.

Darwin, Charles. *Journal of Researches in the Natural History and Geology of the Countries visited during the Voyage of H.M.S. Beagle round the World*. New York, 1890.

Edwards, William Henry. *A Voyage up the River Amazon*. New York, 1847.

Eiby, G. A. *About Earthquakes*. New York, 1957.

Fawcett, P. H. *Lost Trails, Lost Cities*. New York, 1953.

Frezier, Amedee Francois. *A Voyage to the South-Sea and along the Coast of Chili and Peru in the Years 1712, 1713 and 1714*. London, 1717.

Garcilaso de la Vega, El Inca. *The Royal Commentaries of Peru*. London, 1688.

Gregory, Herbert E. *A Geographical Sketch of Titicaca, the Island of the Sun*. American Geographical Society, New York, 1913.

Hagen, Victor W. von (editor). *The Green World of the Naturalists*. New York, 1948.

Harcourt, Raoul d' and Marie d'. *La Musique des Incas et ses survivances*. Paris, 1925.

Herndon, W. L. and L. Gibbon. *Exploration of the Valley of the Amazon*. Washington, 1854.

Herrera y Tordesillas, Antonio de. *The general history of the vast continent and islands of America . . . trans. by John Stevens*. London, 1725–6.

Heyerdahl, Thor. *American Indians in the Pacific*. Chicago, 1953.

Holstein, Otto. "Chan-Chan: Capitol of the Great Chimu," *Geographical Review*, XVII, American Geographical Society, New York, 1927.

Humboldt, Alexander von. *Researches concerning the Institutions and Monuments of the Ancient Inhabitants of America*. Trans. Helen Maria Williams. London, 1814. 2 vols.

————. *Personal Narrative of Travels to the Equinoctial Regions of the New Continent*. London, 1849.

Hutchinson, T. J. *Two Years in Peru with Exploration of its Antiquities*. London, 1873. 2 vols.

Karsten, R. *The Civilization of the South American Indians, with Special Reference to Magic and Religion*. London, 1926.

Keleman, Pal. *Medieval American Art*. New York, 1943. 2 vols.

Keller-Leuzinger, Franz. *The Amazon and Madeira Rivers*. London, 1874.

Kelsey, Vera. *Seven Keys to Brazil*. New York & London, 1941.

Kravigny, Frank W. *The Jungle Route*. New York, 1940.

La Condamine, Charles-Marie de. *Abridged Narrative of Travels Through the Interior of South America*, in *Pinkerton's Voyages and Travels*, Vol. 14. London, 1813.

Lehman, Walter, and Heinrich Doering. *The Art of Old Peru*. New York, 1924.

Mangelsdorf, P. C. and R. G. Reeves. *The Origin of Indian Corn and its Relatives*. Texas Agricultural Experiment Station, Bulletin 574, College Station, May, 1939.

Markham, C. R. *Cuzco & Lima*. London, 1856.

————. *Contributions toward a Grammar and Dictionary of Quichua, the Language of the Incas of Peru*. London, 1864.

————. *The Incas of Peru*. London & New York ,1910.

Mathews, Edward D. *Up the Amazon and Madeira Rivers*. London, 1879.

Means, P. A. *A Study of Ancient Andean Social Institutions*. Transactions of the Connecticut Academy of Arts and Sciences, New Haven, 1925.

————. *Ancient civilizations of the Andes*. New York, 1931.

————. *Fall of the Inca Empire and the Spanish Rule in Peru: 1530–1780*. New York, 1932.

Millar, George. *A Crossbowman's Story of the First Exploration of the Amazon*. New York, 1955.

Montesinos, Fernando. *Memorias Antiguas Historiales del Peru*. Trans. & ed., P. A. Means. London, 1920.

Mortimer, W. G. *Coca, the Divine Plant of the Incas*. New York, 1901.

Mozans, H. J. *Along the Andes and Down the Amazon.* New York & London, 1911.

Murphy, Robert Cushman. "Fisheries Resources in Peru," *Scientific Monthly,* XVI, 1923.

———. *Bird Islands of Peru.* New York, 1925.

———. *Oceanic Birds of South America.* New York, 1936. 2 vols.

Newell, N. D. *Geology of the Lake Titicaca Region, Peru and Bolivia.* Geological Society of America, Memoir 36, New York, 1949.

Ogilvie, Alan G. *Geography of the Central Andes.* American Geographical Society, New York, 1922.

Orton, James. *The Andes and The Amazon.* New York, 1876.

Picart, B. *Ceremonies of the Idolatrous Nations.* London, 1734.

Pizzaro, Pedro. *Relation of the Discovery and Conquest of the Kingdoms of Peru.* New York, 1921.

Posnansky, A. *Tihuanacu. The Cradle of American Man.* (Vols. I & II.) New York, 1945.

———. *Tihuanacu. The Cradle of American Man.* (Vols. III & IV.) La Paz, 1957.

Price, Willard. *The Amazing Amazon.* New York, 1952.

Prodgers, C. H. *Adventures in Bolivia.* New York, 1922.

Rivero, M. E., and J. J. von Tschudi. *Peruvian Antiquities.* New York, 1853.

Roosevelt, Theodore. *Through the Brazilian Wilderness.* New York, 1914.

Sauer, Carl. *American Agricultural Origins: A Consideration of Nature and Culture,* in *Essays in Anthropology.* Berkeley, 1936.

Saville, M. H. *Antiquities of Manabi.* New York, 1907–10. 2 vols.

Southey, Robert. *History of Brazil.* London, 1810–19. 3 vols.

Spruce, Richard. *Notes of a Botanist on the Amazon and Andes* (ed. A. R. Wallace). London, 1908. 2 vols.

Squier, E. G. *Peru: Incidents of Travel & Exploration in the Land of the Incas.* New York, 1877.

Stevenson, W. B. *A Historical and Descriptive Narrative of Twenty Years' Residence in South America.* London, 1825. 3 vols.

Steward, Julian H. (editor). *Handbook of South American Indians.* Bureau of American Ethnology, Washington, 1946. 6 vols.

Sutcliffe, Thomas. *Sixteen Years in Chile & Peru.* London, 1841.

Temple, Edmund. *Travels in Various Parts of Peru.* London, 1830.

Tschudi, J. J. von. *Travels in Peru.* New York, 1854.

Uhle, Max. *Pachacamac.* Philadelphia, 1903.

Up De Graff, F. W. *Head Hunters of the Amazon.* New York, 1923.

Verrill, A. H. *The American Indian, North, South and Central America*. New York, 1927.

————. *Old civilizations of the New World*. New York, 1929.

Villavicencio, Victor L. *La Vida Sexual del Indígena Peruano*. Club del Libro Peruano, Lima, 1942.

Wallace, A. R. *Narrative of Travels on the Amazon and Rio Negro*. London, 1889.

Whymper, Edward. *Travels Amongst the Great Andes of the Equator*. London, 1892.

Zarate, Agustin. *The Discoverie and Conquest of the Prouvinces of Peru . . . Written in foure bookes, by Augustine Sarate. (Translated out of the Spanish tongue, by F. Nicholas)*. London, 1581.

HENRY FORD

Anonymous, "Mr. Ford Doesn't Care," *Fortune Magazine*, December, 1933.

Arnold, Horace L., and Fay L. Faurote. *Ford Methods and Ford Shops*. Engineering Magazine Co., 1915.

Bennett, Harry. *We Never Called Him Henry*. New York, 1951.

Benson, Allan L. *The New Henry Ford*. New York & London, 1923.

Bowie, Beverley M. "The Past is Present in Greenfield Village," *National Geographic Magazine*, Washington, July, 1958.

Burlingame, Roger. *Henry Ford, A Great Life in Brief*. New York, 1955.

Ford, Henry, and Samuel Crowther. *My Life and Work*. Garden City, 1924.

Garrett, Garet. *The Wild Wheel*. New York, 1952.

Lochner, Louis P. *Henry Ford: America's Don Quixote*. New York, 1925.

Marquis, Samuel S. *Henry Ford: an Interpretation*. Boston, 1923.

McCarthy, Joe, "The Ford Family," *Holiday Magazine*, Philadelphia, June–Sept., 1957.

McGuffey, William H. *Eclectic Fourth Reader*. New York & Cincinnati, 1849.

Merz, Charles. *And Then Came Ford*. New York, 1929.

Nevins, Allan, and Frank Ernest Hill. *Ford: the Times, the Man and the Company*. New York, 1954.

————. *Ford: Expansion and Challenge: 1915–1933*. New York, 1957.

Nowlin, William. *The Bark Covered House*. Chicago, 1937.

Petersham, Maud and Miska. *The Rooster Crows: A Book of American Rhymes and Jingles*. New York, 1953.

Pierson, George W. (editor). *Toqueville and Beaumont in America*. New York, 1938.

Pound, Arthur. *Detroit, Dynamic City*. New York, 1940.

Richards, William C. *The Last Billionaire*. New York, 1948.

Ruddiman, Margaret, "Memories of My Brother Henry Ford," *Michigan History,* Lansing, Sept. 1953.

Simonds, William A. *Henry Ford: His Life, His Work, His Genius*. New York, 1943.

————. *Henry Ford and Greenfield Village*. New York, 1938.

Sinclair, Upton. *The Flivver King*. Pasadena, 1937.

Stern, Philip Van Doren. *Tin Lizzie*. New York, 1955.

Sward, Keith. *The Legend of Henry Ford*. New York, 1948.

Wilson, Edmund, "The Despot of Dearborn," *Scribner's Magazine,* New York, July 1931.